D0763666

DOUBLE VISION

REFLECTIONS OF A
BICULTURAL CANADIAN

DOUBLE VISION
Reflections of
a Bicultural Canadian

Lyse Champagne

KEY PORTER·BOOKS

Copyright © 1990 by Lyse Champagne

All rights reserved. No part of this work covered by the copyrights hereon may be reproduced or used in any form or by any means — graphic, electronic or mechanical, including photocopying, recording, taping or information storage and retrieval systems — without the prior written permission of the publisher.

Canadian Cataloguing in Publication Data

Champagne, Lyse
    Double vision : reflections of a bicultural Canadian

ISBN 1-55013-266-0

1. Canada – English-French relations.
2. Biculturalism – Canada.   3. Bilingualism –
Canada.   I. Title.

FC144.C48 1990   971.064   C90-094872-8
F1027.C48 1990

Key Porter Books Limited
70 The Esplanade
Toronto, Ontario
Canada M5E 1R2

Typesetting: Pixel Graphics, Inc.

∞ Printed on acid-free paper
Printed and bound in Canada

90 91 92 93 94 95 6 5 4 3 2 1

Contents

Introduction / 1

1. Living Between the Two Solitudes / 7
2. Growing Up in the Other Ontario / 19
3. Rednecks in Stereo / 33
4. Bits and Pieces of the Past / 45
5. Separation Anxiety / 57
6. Swimming in Meech Lake / 67
7. The Legacy of Babel / 77
8. The Politics of Language / 89
9. Double Duty in the Public Service / 101
10. Solitudes, Mosaics, and Melting Pots / 113
11. The Politics of Otherness / 125
12. Living with Cultural Schizophrenia / 135

Conclusion / 145

À Marguerite Allard Champagne, en souvenir de son amour et de son courage.

To Marguerite Allard Champagne, in memory of her love and courage.

Introduction

I AM A CANADIAN, A BICULTURAL CANADIAN. A simple enough statement, but in a country obsessed with bilingualism and multiculturalism, a political one. We are expected to provide more precise linguistic and ethnic identification than that. So I must confess that I am a French Canadian and, to satisfy the regionalists, that I come from Ontario.

Born in one solitude, living in the other, I travel mostly in between. It is an interesting, sometimes exciting journey, but a lonely one. Not belonging is the price I pay for being bilingual and bicultural, for refusing to stay on my side of the great Canadian cultural divide.

English-speaking public servants who struggle with French verbs to keep their jobs will scoff at the price. And the Québécois who want French-only signs will shrug. A Gallic shrug, of course. Native Canadians can hardly be expected to choose sides in a quarrel that excludes them – as it excludes Canadians from other ethnic backgrounds, recent immigrants, and refugees seeking safety rather than special status.

My dilemma, however, is real enough. Take Bill 178, the whole issue of bilingual signs. Inside versus outside. I tell people I don't care, one way or another, that it's a Québec issue, and that I'm not from Québec. But I can never get away with it.

Because my mother tongue is French, my friends in Québec expect me to support every measure they take to protect their language and culture. My language and culture. Because I am so fluent in English, my friends in English Canada assume that I share their outrage over Bill 178. I learned the "real" language of the country, didn't I? Smartest move I ever made, wasn't it?

I refuse to be drawn into their arguments, their assumptions. I don't even tell them that I understand both sides. Because in this debate, you're not supposed to understand both sides, you're supposed to take sides.

Bill 178 is just one incarnation of the French-English

question, a question that permeates my life, as it permeates Canadian history. For me and people like me, the day-to-day realities of living between cultures often outweigh the big issues like the Meech Lake Accord, sovereignty-association, and minority language rights.

"You don't know how lucky you are to be bilingual, to be able to switch from one language to the other like that. It's so easy for you. You don't even have an accent or anything," English Canadians often tell me.

Easy? Lucky? I don't remember having any choice in the matter. Do they think I was born with a bilingual spoon in my mouth? That my fluency and my ability to write professionally in two languages just happened? That it required no personal effort or commitment on my part?

And that comment about my accent, it's like telling someone he really doesn't look Jewish, or telling someone else she doesn't sound like a "foreigner."

"Just remember who you really are. Don't betray us," French Canadians warn me, knowing the word *betray* will score as surely as Mario Lemieux will.

They too have noticed that I speak English without an accent, but they don't mention it. They don't have to, their disapproval is obvious enough, in their eyes, in their tone of voice.

Welcome to the contradictions of a bicultural life:

It's feeling guilty reading the English list of ingredients on my box of cereal in the morning.

It's reminding my son to speak French to his French friends, although he'd much rather talk to them in English.

It's being incapable of singing "O Canada" in English even though I know the lyrics.

It's being ashamed of French Canadians who are talking loudly during the keynote address at an annual banquet at the Royal York. It's being ashamed of English Canadians who are doing the same thing during a presentation at the Château Frontenac.

It's being insulted when I'm served in English first at a Montréal hotel.

It's doing my public service job twice, once in English, once in French.

It's always having to juggle two professional vocabularies at work so that I can switch (effortlessly, of course) from one official language to the other.

It's knowing the government is spending thousands of dollars to teach anglophone public servants to say *bonjour* and not a penny to help their already bilingual public servants (mostly francophones) maintain the integrity of their mother tongue.

It's listening to Gordon Lightfoot, Rita McNeil, Blue Rodeo, and k.d. lang as well as Gilles Vigneault, Pauline Julien, Mitsou, Hart Rouge, and Edith Butler.

It's watching "Le Point" and "The Journal," reading *Le Devoir* and the *Globe and Mail*, listening to "Morningside" and "Les Actualités."

It's seeing Québec films like *Le Déclin de l'empire américain* and *Un Zoo la nuit* filed in the foreign film section of the video store.

It's realizing that most of my English-speaking friends have heard of *Uncle Tom's Cabin* (an American pre-Civil War classic on slavery) but not *The White Niggers of America* (a book about the inferior status of French Canadians written more than a hundred years later).

It's knowing I've read books by Margaret Atwood, Robertson Davies, Alice Munro, Bharati Mukherjee, and Josef Škvorecký in English when most of my English-speaking friends have never read Antonine Maillet, Anne Hébert, Michel Tremblay, or Yves Beauchemin, even in translation.

You've heard enough? You think it's just the same old garbage about the two solitudes not understanding each other? (Recycled garbage, at that?)

But it's not about the two solitudes not understanding each other, it's about understanding the two solitudes. Knowing both of them intimately – too intimately, perhaps. And not wanting to choose between them.

The debate over the Meech Lake Accord has polarized Canadians and triggered an unprecedented outpouring of anti-French, anti-English sentiment, proving once and for all how little we do understand one another.

You've heard from the politicians, the constitutional experts, the academics, the pollsters, and the journalists. You've listened to the promoters, the compromisers, and the rednecks on both sides. I would like to add another voice, a different point of view. The view from the middle. As in "caught in the middle."

I am not an expert; personal experience is my only expertise. I do not have a professional opinion, just a very personal one. I do not have any answers, only the same questions you have about our country and the people who live in it.

Opinion, by its very nature, is subjective. So are the memories that inspired much of this book. Although the anecdotes are based on actual incidents, names have been changed and, in some cases, details altered to protect the privacy of those involved. I am sharing these anecdotes and observations because I believe they are not unique, that they reflect the reality of many biculturals in this country, whether they are French-English or another combination.

Expect contradictions, because living two lives is a contradiction. Expect compromises, because living in two cultures requires compromise. Expect the unexpected, because living a double life brings much that is unexpected.

Maybe I will say something that will surprise you, something that will challenge your assumptions about this country, about the people who live in it. About how people learn to belong or not belong.

Because belonging is everything, isn't it?

1. Living Between the Two Solitudes

A bluff in northern Iceland, overlooking the Arctic Ocean, as close as I have ever come to the ends of the earth. The grey skies have turned to silver, giving literal meaning to the expression *clouds with silver linings*. The water is very still and glassy. It doesn't look like the Arctic Ocean at all, but a lake in northern Ontario, except that there are no trees.

I fiddle with my camera indecisively, trying to figure out how best to capture the shimmering silveriness in front of me. The bus driver has kindly agreed to stop here for ten minutes, although it isn't on our itinerary. He dutifully informs us that the Arctic Circle is fifty miles to the north, and we dutifully stare in that direction.

Yvon, one of the Canadians on the tour, is hovering over me as usual. I guess I should say hovering under me, since Yvon is very short and I am very tall. He is always asking questions about my camera. Which f-stop I'm using. What speed film. I don't have the heart to tell him that the equipment is borrowed and the camera is on automatic most of the time.

Not wanting to waste the few remaining minutes I have left, I mutter something about changing the lens. I use the word *lentille,* which is French for lens but not for camera lens, which is *objectif*. This type of mistake happens a lot when you speak two languages on a regular basis.

"You should be ashamed of yourself, using an anglicism like that. You of all people should have respect for language," Yvon remonstrates, "especially your own language. And you call yourself a writer!"

Thank God, I never told him I write in English!

I glare at him and go back to my viewfinder. But I'm too upset to concentrate on the layers of light.

What does it matter what that self-important busybody thinks of my French? It's not the first time I've heard that little sermon and it won't be the last. I hear it all the time, back home.

But that's just it. I'm on a remote bluff in northern Iceland, thousands of miles from home. Is there no escape from the two solitudes, even at the ends of the earth?

* * *

FOR PEOPLE WHO SPEAK ONLY ONE LANGUAGE, the language of the majority, this incident may seem trivial, inconsequential. So how can I explain it? Why do I even want to?

For the children of immigrants, such encounters are all too common. They are scolded in much the same way when they go home to visit their parents or stop to chat in the old neighbourhood. Scolded for mixing English words with the ones from the old country, for forgetting the old ways, for rejecting the old quarrels.

Only for me, it doesn't just happen when I visit my family or my old neighbourhood; it can happen anywhere where there are Canadians. English Canadians who think French is being shoved down their throats. French Canadians who think I've sold out.

Sometimes, I feel like an immigrant in my own country. Which is the way a friend of mine describes the way she feels whenever she visits the country of her childhood.

"At first, everything seems so familiar, exactly as I remember it. But within days, I start to feel unfamiliar, strange, out of place, like an immigrant in my own country."

I haven't emigrated, I still live in the city where I was born. But Yvon's self-righteous little sermon, thousands of miles from home, made me realize that I had indeed emigrated. That the country I now live in is not the same as his, although it shares the same physical boundaries. And because the emigration is sociological rather than geographic, I can never escape, I must always explain. Explain why I left the country of my childhood.

Immigrants have to explain only when they return to the old country for a visit. (Why do you have to live so far away?

Don't you realize how much the family misses you?) They, in turn, apply "cultural" pressure on their own children who are growing up Canadian. (Why don't you go out with a nice Italian girl? Why don't you speak to me in Chinese? In India, a good girl would not choose the man she wishes to marry.)

In most cases, immigrants have decided to start a new life in another country. But for me, there never was a decision. My biculturalism just happened. Gradually, over time.

Although my emigration was not voluntary, I did choose to stay. To live in two cultures instead of one, and in so doing, to incur the wrath of those French Canadians who still view the English as the "enemy." To them my "emigration" is a betrayal, a rejection of my culture, their culture.

And that is why another French Canadian can lash out at me in Iceland, thousands of miles from home. And why I react with feelings of guilt and shame.

You've probably noticed by now that I call myself a French Canadian and not a Franco-Ontarian.

What did I do, sleep through the Quiet Revolution?

Acadiens, Franco-Ontariens, Franco-Manitobains...we all have our little niches now. For some of us, however, it just means the hyphen has moved from the national label to the provincial one.

To call oneself Québécois or Québécoise instead of French Canadian is to move from a minority situation (within Canada) to a majority situation (within Québec). But since I am not from Québec, I can't benefit from this kind of minority-to-majority shift in identification. That leaves me with Franco-Ontarian, francophone, or *francophone-hors-Québec*, none of which appeals to me. So I settle for French Canadian, even though it's no longer fashionable.

I rarely call myself a francophone. To me, it's a linguistic designation meaning French-speaking, not the synonym for French or French Canadian that it is fast becoming.

Let me give you an example.

In Sherbrooke a few years ago, I went on an organized heritage tour. Our guide was fluently bilingual and quite knowledgeable about the history and architecture of his city. After taking us around the city and showing us two beautiful churches and a run-down hotel where Duplessis had once made a speech, he stopped in front of a handsomely restored *canadienne* house. He pointed out its special features, the sloping roof, the gabled windows, the wide veranda.

"All in all," he said, "this house is a splendid example of francophone architecture." I cringed at the word. Farther up the street, he showed us two examples of "anglophone" architecture. English-speaking and French-speaking houses? I bet they don't talk to each other.

All the labels notwithstanding (see how handy a notwithstanding clause can be), there are really only two types of French Canadians. Those who live in Québec and those who don't. There's even an organization for those of us who don't: the *Fédération des francophones hors Québec*. Sounds like a banana republic in exile to me. Why should I identify myself as a *francophone-hors-Québec*? I don't see my Québec cousins calling themselves *francophones-hors-France*. Or Canadians calling themselves non-Americans.

Hubert Aquin, a Québécois writer, coined the expression *fatigue culturelle* to describe the weariness that results from having to struggle to preserve one's culture. If the Québécois suffer from cultural fatigue when their language and culture are in a majority situation in the province, then French Canadians living in English provinces must suffer from cultural exhaustion. For they are trying to preserve their language and culture, fighting to improve, maintain, or regain their rights, while living in an often hostile environment.

It's so easy to sit in judgement on the thousands who have been assimilated or acculturated over the years. Assimilated and acculturated are polite, sociological terms, used by polite sociologists. *Sold out* is the expression more commonly used –

less politely of course. I have been called a *vendue* many times for choosing to live in both cultures instead of one.

It's easy to forget how much harder the struggle has been outside Québec. When I think of the high-quality education I received (which I owe to the dedication of my teachers and my parents), of the excellent French I was taught (although many textbooks were in English only), of the French life that I lived right in the middle of an English city, I realize how much of an effort it was on the part of individuals. A constant, daily effort. When I think of going to the public library and scrounging through the motley collection of French books, held together with red or green tape, looking for a title I hadn't read six times, I realize how miraculous it is that the language survived at all.

So when I hear a Québécois laugh at the kind of French we speak in Ontario, Alberta, or any other province, I just ask him how much of a personal effort he had to make to preserve his language while he was growing up.

Québec's language policies over the last twenty years have come as a surprise to many Canadians. As a betrayal. They wonder why Canada should be officially bilingual if Québec wants to be unilingual. Contrary to what many Canadians believe, official bilingualism was neither the brainchild of the Québec government nor something the people of Québec demanded. It was a federal solution to a constitutional problem.

Québec never insisted on Canada-wide bilingualism, only federal services in French for its inhabitants. These could have been provided by the federal public servants already working in Montréal and Quebec City, with some additional arrangements to cover programs that were administered only from Ottawa. The real problem, in Ottawa's view, was that Québec wanted more power in areas that were clearly federal, such as immigration and communications. What Québec wanted, and still wants, is equality, not with other provinces but with the rest of Canada. That is what the concept of dual nationhood entails.

Bilingualism is a two-edged sword for a linguistic minority

(in this case, Québec within Canada) because the use of two languages often results in more assimilation, more acculturation in the community with the minority language. Bilingualism can be the Trojan horse in a linguistic struggle: once the horse is allowed in, the battle is lost.

Québec has therefore continued to fashion its own language policies, in spite of the official bilingualism policy of the federal government.

The trouble with being French in this country, particularly if you live in an English province, is that you are held personally responsible for any action taken on behalf of French language and culture. When legislation is passed in Québec (where I don't even reside), or the prime minister and ten provincial premiers sign an accord at Meech Lake recognizing Québec as a distinct society, or the Supreme Court decides for or against a province on a question of minority language rights, I am expected to defend it. It is, of course, assumed that I agree with the legislation/accord/decision in question.

I don't go around collaring the English Canadians I know and berating them for bills passed in Saskatchewan and Alberta that make English the official language of those provinces. I know they don't live there and I don't hold them responsible just because they're English-speaking. Nor would I hold them responsible for the actions of any other English-Canadian premier in Canada.

The fact that I am French Canadian does not make me an automatic supporter of the Official Languages Act in Canada, Bill 101 (Charte de la langue) in Québec, or Bill 8 (French Language Services Act) in Ontario. Being a strong supporter of minority rights does not make me party to every attempt to legislate them.

Living between two cultures keeps me busy enough without being drawn into every single debate on Meech Lake, Bill 8, French-only signs, or the plight of English-only public servants.

Am I living in both cultures or between them? It's hard to

say. Most of the time I feel as if I'm living in both cultures. But when there is conflict – and there has been much conflict lately – I feel more as if I'm living between them.

Let me try a couple of metaphors.

Assise entre deux chaises. Roughly translates as *sitting between two chairs*. There's a similar English expression, *caught between two stools*.

The trouble with sitting between two chairs is that you end up on the floor – which is not the most comfortable place. You like both chairs, although for different reasons. One is elegant, a little ornate; the other, practical and versatile.

You get to spend time on each chair, although you're never allowed to stay for very long. Something always happens, and you end up on the floor again. And while you're on the floor, you can see the underside of the chairs, the way the material is fraying on this one, the slightly crooked frame, the unfinished underside of the other.

Don't like that metaphor? What about this one?

You're at a flower show. You see a beautiful flower. Well, it's not really beautiful, not when you look at it closely. It's odd in a familiar, not exotic, sort of way.

You check the name tag, more than a little curious. *Marguerose*. What the hell is a *marguerose*? Well, the gardener is anxious to explain, it's a cross between a daisy and a rose. Daisy is *marguerite* in French you see, hence *marguerose*.

But that's ridiculous. Who would ever cross a rose and a daisy? Talk about two flowers that don't go together. You walk on, annoyed at having spent even a moment looking at that ridiculous hybrid.

We have trouble with hybrids. Especially in human nature. We like our differences to be sharp, not blurred. Otherwise they're not differences are they?

I'm a cultural hybrid. Although purists will insist I can't use the word hybrid, since my parents were both French Canadian and I was raised as one. I'm an impostor. A daisy posing as a rose or a rose posing as a daisy.

I live in both cultures by choice, although I had no choice in the beginning. But then none of us do in the beginning. We're born where we're born. We don't choose our parents, our mother tongue, our social standing.

I think the most difficult aspect of this kind of life is the double vision you develop. Second sight, some people would call it, enamoured by the possibilities of dual perception. But I prefer the term *double vision*, because seeing both sides has a tendency to blur things. And give one a headache.

Let's look at Bill 178 with double vision.

I know only too well why my Québec cousins want to protect their language. I grew up French in English Ontario. Every printed word around me was in a language other than my own. From the street sign on the corner to bus schedules, to the labels on the bread, milk, and other foodstuffs I picked up for my mother at the local A & P, everything was in English. My private world was French (home, school, church, community centre); my public world was English (public transportation, health care, shopping).

So I understand why my Québec cousins would like to surround themselves with French-only signs. They are an important symbol, an affirmation of self, and certainly no worse than the English-only signs that used to predominate in Québec.

I understand all this, I even sympathize, but I don't agree. Signs are supposed to communicate, and unilingual signs communicate a message that is opposite to what a shopkeeper is trying to do, which is to sell. Why can't an English bookstore have a bilingual sign? Why can't a Chinese grocery? Or a Portuguese bakery?

I happen to think that legislating how shopkeepers attract their customers is ridiculous. That Bill 178 is reactionary and unnecessary.

Then I hear a member of the Equality party during Québec's last provincial election proudly proclaim that he has lived in Québec for sixty years and has never spoken French. What kind of "equality" does he stand for? Would he like the English language to be treated with the same contempt he has shown for French, the majority language in his province?

I read about the father who took his children out of French classes at a Regina school to protest the passing of Bill 178. Does he realize his province has declared itself unilingual and limited the rights of the French in Saskatchewan?

I hear about the Ottawa alderman who could not support any new initiatives in the city's official languages policy because of the passage of Bill 178 in Ontario's neighbouring province. Where was his indignation when Ontario's other neighbouring province limited the rights of French Canadians there?

Then I start to wonder: Why do the English, who have more rights in Québec than the French do in any other province in Canada, rate so much higher in the moral-outrage department? Why are French-only signs in Québec more deplorable than English-only education in other provinces? Doesn't anyone realize how unalike they are, the English minority in Québec and the French minorities in the rest of Canada, how unequal?

No, I don't like Bill 178, but I also don't like the company I'm keeping when I denounce it.

If every issue has two sides, what happens when you have double vision? You see everything in quadruplicate.

I find that living between two cultures has opened my eyes to the experience of other Canadians, the ones we've excluded from our two-founding-nations scenario: the aboriginal peoples who were here long before there was a Canada, the Ukrainians who settled the West, the descendants of other immigrants who answered Clifford Sifton's call, the Asians we let in to build our railways (and the ones we turned away), the Japanese Canadians we interned in the Second World War, all the immigrants who have come since the war.

I cannot presume to know or understand what these people or their descendants have experienced. But I recognize their contribution to the development of this country, their right to participate in the shaping of Canada's future.

As long as we remain obsessed with the two solitudes, we are excluding all these Canadians, we are denying them their rightful place. I know I'm not supposed to think this way, that I'm expected to focus my energies on my own minority. But I can't, my double vision won't let me.

I don't always have double vision. On some issues, I wear my French glasses; on others, my English glasses. But when I try to see myself as a Canadian, I have to wear both pairs.

Take off the second pair of glasses, the French tell me. No, take off the first pair, say the English. But it's not that simple, for the glasses are only an analogy, and the double vision is not. It is very real. I can no longer see through the eyes of my childhood. I can only see through the eyes of my experience.

2. Growing Up in the Other Ontario

T he day is perfect, just as I prayed it would be. Last year it rained and the procession had to be postponed until the following Sunday. Then it was so hot people were fainting all over the place.

I'm ready and waiting, have been for hours. I'm wearing my school uniform and, for the first time, the blue and white *foulard* of a *croisée* (a school club named after the Crusades). My new *béret*, which I've adjusted and readjusted in the hall mirror, completes the outfit.

I sit on the front porch railing, trying to look solemn, while my mother takes a picture with her Brownie camera.

"Don't look so serious. God never said you couldn't smile," she teases me, unimpressed by my attempts at solemnity.

Finally it is time to walk to church and join the ranks of the *Fête-Dieu* procession. This is the first time I'm taking part in this procession; I've only ever watched it before. When I join my classmates, we admire each other's curls and fuss with each other's *foulards*.

Our teacher herds us to the front of the procession.

"Now remember. Hold your head up, keep your shoulders back, look straight ahead. Don't try to find your parents in the crowd, and don't wave to your friends. Show respect for the Holy Sacrament."

It takes a while for all the groups to form behind us, but we finally get under way. Although I am dutifully following our teacher's instructions, my classmates are giggling and waving at their friends and families, as if they were walking in a parade instead of a religious procession.

The view is lousy. All I see is the backs of the girls in front of me. I wish I were on the sidelines again, watching row after row of people walking by. The Boy Scouts and the Girl Guides, proud in their uniforms. The nuns, the brothers, and the priests in their long brown robes. The adults wearing the various *foulards* of their organizations.

I miss finding my mother's face, my father's, recognizing

my aunts and uncles, my older cousins. And I miss the sunlight glinting on the white and gold vestments, the wind unfurling the various flags and banners.

Slowly we wend our way through the parish, stopping for a few minutes at two private homes. Every year two homes are chosen and temporary altars set up on their porches to receive the Holy Sacrament. It is considered quite an honour. This year, the home of one of my friends has been chosen.

We find our way back to Wellington Street, which has been closed to traffic, down Parkdale Avenue to Scott Street, and up my own street to the boys' school. We assemble in the schoolyard for readings and prayers.

I kneel on the pavement, confident that my new tights will not suffer any damage. God would not let that happen, not when I'm praying like this.

We are each given a special token to commemorate the day, a holy image in a little plastic pouch with a blue ribbon. I already have this particular image but not sealed in plastic like this one is.

I walk home with my mother and father. Although our house is just half a block away, it takes us a while to get home as my parents stop at almost every house to chat with the neighbours sitting on their front porch.

❊ ❊ ❊

EVERY TIME I WALK THROUGH THE STREETS OF my childhood, I am surprised. Surprised that the street signs, the houses (even the one where I spent thirteen years of my life), the corner store (always sporting a new name, it seems), and the park do not seem as real as my recollections.

The trouble with childhood is that we tend to think of it as a place, a place we like to go back to, a place that was safe (for those of us who had safe childhoods). But like the rest of our past, childhood isn't a place, just a jumble of memories, highly subjective and elusive. Although these memories are very real, they are seldom accurate or complete. What we remember about our childhood says more about what we've become than what actually happened to us. And what actually happened can never be confirmed, only imagined and reconstructed.

I want to take you for a walk through my childhood, down the streets of my old neighbourhood, to a world that has disappeared forever. The time: late fifties to mid-sixties.

I lived an essentially French life in an English province, when Ottawa was, with the exception of a few isolated pockets, unilingual English. There were English people on my street, all through my neighbourhood, but I knew them only by name. They did not belong to my world. My social unit wasn't the neighbourhood but the parish. I was twenty-two years old before I found out that my old neighbourhood was called Hintonburg. To me it was always *la paroisse Saint-François d'Assise*, Saint-François for short. It was the second-largest French parish in Ottawa, second only to Notre-Dame in Lower Town.

The parish was a self-contained unit. A church, three schools, a community centre, a variety of stores and businesses, a *caisse populaire*, a public library, even a funeral parlour. The parish was where we lived, worshipped, went to school, shopped, and socialized.

The church was very central to our lives. Sunday Mass was the main event, although many parishioners went to Mass every day. There were special devotions and rituals all year round, novenas, the month of May (*mois de Marie*), stations of the cross, major feast days like Christmas and Easter. Our church, like churches, synagogues, temples everywhere, was where all the stages of life were ritualized – birth, marriage, death.

Saint-François was the parish where my grandparents were born, grew up, married, and raised their nine children. They ran a general store on Hinchey Street and then a dry goods store on Wellington, right across from the church.

Although they moved away to the suburbs for a few years at the end of their lives, they never really left the parish, they never belonged anywhere else. Since most of their children settled in the parish, their grandchildren were the third (and last) generation of the family to be born and raised there.

The priests lived in a monastery next to the church, and the nuns and brothers who taught in our schools also lived in the parish. There was no clear dividing line between church and school. The events of one mixed with the events of the other.

Social activities were held in the church basement (bingo every Tuesday night, teas, bake sales, school plays, award presentations, slide shows, and films) or at the community centre adjacent to the presbytery. Every year we had an outdoor bazaar on the church grounds, a mini-fair, with a small Ferris wheel, a merry-go-round, cotton candy and candy apples, popcorn, and craft displays. This was not out in the country but in a working-class city neighbourhood.

Various religious and social clubs (*le Tiers Ordre, Fédération des femmes canadienne-françaises, la Ligue du Sacré-Coeur*) met in the church basement or at the community centre, as did the Boy Scouts and Girl Guides. The community centre had a bowling alley and a gym. My parents bowled there every Friday night in a parish league, along with my grandparents, aunts, and uncles.

The stores on our portion of Wellington Street were not frequented only by French Canadians. Some were owned by parishioners, others were not. There were chain stores like the A & P and United Stores (a five-and-dime), but also lots of local businesses – a hardware store (Quincaillerie Ménard), a jeweller (Bijouterie Lavoie), a men's wear store (Rolly's), a bicycle shop (Saint-Louis), a pharmacy (Barrette), my grandparents' dry goods store, and so on.

English was all around. The sign at the corner of my street said Stirling Avenue. All the street names were English –

Pinhey, Merton, Armstrong, Carruthers, Scott, Wellington –
except for one, which was Ladouceur. Everything we bought
at the A & P had English labels. I don't recall if the hand-written
signs in the meat department were in French or not, but the
cashiers in the store always spoke to us in French.

I don't know exactly how I learned English or how much I
spoke it. My memories of those years are all French. I know
that I took English in school and that the nuns were as thorough
as they were with everything else and we had grammar drills
and spelling bees in English.

I understood English, there's no doubt about that. I was an
avid reader and almost lived at the library. When I had read and
reread every French book in the place, I started in on the
English ones. The first serious English book I remember
reading was *Great Expectations* by Charles Dickens.

In grade seven, I started to read Trixie Belden and Nancy
Drew books. Since our library didn't carry them, I borrowed
them from my friends or bought them second-hand. I had been
brought up on French books from France, so it was a treat to
read about kids that lived North American lives – although
their lives were very different from mine.

I don't know what year we first had a television set, but
1954 seems to ring a bell. We watched television in French and
English, but mostly in French. Every night, my mother would
watch one of her *téléromans*, something like a soap opera.
Monday night it was "Les Belles Histoires des pays d'en-haut,"
which had been on radio before that. Then there was "La
Famille Plouffe" on Wednesday nights, a program that was also
dubbed into English and very popular in English Canada.
"Côte de Sable" was set in Ottawa's Sandy Hill during the war.
These were low-budget Radio-Canada productions. We also
watched "The Ed Sullivan Show" on Sunday nights and, eventually, "Bonanza." "La Soirée du hockey" was sacred in our
house on Saturday night (my mother was a rabid fan).

The world I remember is a French world, also a Catholic

one. I was very devout, going to Mass every day during Lent, to prayers every night during May (*le mois de Marie*). I couldn't be an altar boy like my brothers, but I was in church as often as, if not more often than they. And the world of the church was exclusively Latin and French. It was a world where English just didn't exist.

I understood English, but that didn't mean I could speak it all that well. I had very little practice. Forays outside the parish often resulted in misunderstandings. Like the first time I went to a shopping centre in the suburbs and tried to get off a bus without paying the zone fare (an extra five cents in the outlying areas of the city). The bus driver yelled at me, and although I dropped five cents into the fare box, I still didn't understand what it was for. I tried to explain that I wasn't trying to cheat, but he didn't like my accented English. He called me a stupid frog and told me to get off his bus.

It is my first recollection of being called a frog. I wasn't aware until then that it was an insulting term for French Canadian. I had heard *Frenchie* but not *frog*. I walked around the new shopping centre more than a little bewildered. I still didn't know what the five cents was for, a special fare because I didn't live in the suburbs?

French was so much the norm in my life that in grade seven, when I was twelve, I ran home from school to tell my mother that there was an English girl in my class. "Her name is Pegg-ee," I said, hardly able to contain my excitement about this exotic creature. Twenty years later, my son comes home from school and nonchalantly tells me he has a new friend from Djibouti, without mentioning that he's black.

The same year that Peggy came to my school, one of my uncles married an English Canadian. She was also Protestant, but that didn't seem to be as much of a problem (everyone assumed she would convert).

My parents always spoke English in front of her, as did my aunts and uncles, but I'm sure she felt left out all the same. It would have been hard for a shy country girl to sit in a crowd of boisterous French Canadians and not feel left out. A few years later, another English-speaking aunt appeared on the scene, and the two "outsiders" were soon partners in isolation.

Today, newcomers to the family who don't speak French no longer get special treatment. French is the language spoken at family gatherings, and the accommodation provided by my mother's generation has all but disappeared.

My ex-sister-in-law complained that our family functions were "too French," although everyone who spoke directly to her always did so in English. She didn't want us to speak French, although the French-English ratio was something like ten to one.

On the one hand, I'm glad we now feel confident enough to speak our own language, an option English Canadians have always exercised. But I feel sorry for those who are left out, even though I know some of them have carved out their own isolation.

The kids I grew up with learned English the way I did. On the street, at school, from television, on the job. In the late sixties and early seventies, particularly after the FLQ Crisis, many of them moved to Québec (across the river from Ottawa), to "live in French." They said they were tired of compromising, of being treated like second-class citizens. They wanted their children to grow up in a French environment, which they felt was no longer possible in Ontario.

Their children are now grown and none of them speak English with the fluency of their parents. Some don't speak it at all. I wonder what they will choose for their own children.

Coming back to my own childhood. I was an excellent student, and my favourite subjects were French and history. A potent combination, given the emphasis we French Canadians place on our history, particularly the history of our struggle against the English.

Being French, being Canadian, being Catholic, it was all bound together. Loyalty was everything. Belonging was everything.

I have a yellowed newspaper clipping describing an awards ceremony in the basement of my parish church in February of 1958. The awards, for excellence in French, were handed out to a student in each grade, including kindergarten (excellence in French could not be rewarded too early). I was one of the proud recipients, representing the second grade. I was seven years old.

First we swore allegiance to the flag and sang a patriotic song "Le drapeau canadien." Then we watched a sketch in which Her Majesty the French Language chased the unjust Regulation 17 (see chapter 4). This was followed by a few folk songs and the presentation of the prizes. The reporter summed up the evening as patriotic and an affirmation of the French soul. Being French, being Canadian, being Catholic. All bound together.

I don't remember swearing allegiance to the flag (I thought only Americans did that) or the sketch about Regulation 17. All I remember is being nudged onto the stage to receive a trophy with a tiny red, white, and blue ribbon tied to one of the handles. My name was engraved on a piece of black plastic that was inserted in two little slits. I played with the piece of plastic until it snapped in two and my mother put the trophy away in her purse.

In grade eight, I represented my school in the regional finals of *le Concours de français*. This unique Franco-Ontarian ritual was a province-wide competition in French literature, composition, spelling, handwriting, reading, elocution, recitation, and oral improvisation.

I worked very hard to prepare for these three days of competition. Grammar and spelling drills, diction lessons. Oral improvisations. I rehearsed my recitation, a fable from

Lafontaine, "Le renard et le corbaud." I still recall the opening lines: "Maître Corbaud, sur un arbre perché, tenait en son bec un fromage…"

To participate in this competition was the ultimate challenge, the culmination of years of intense indoctrination. SOYEZ FIERS DE VOTRE LANGUE (Be proud of your language) we were exhorted from banners hanging at the school, in the church basement, and at the community centre.

We were taught that French was the most beautiful language in the world. The most precise. The most romantic. The language of diplomacy. Of culture. French *was* our culture. To betray the language was to betray the culture.

And so to participate in this competition was more than an honour, it was a sacred duty. To demonstrate that French was still alive in Ontario, in all its beauty and glory.

My mother bought me a new uniform – navy tunic and white blouse – although I would be graduating from the primary level in a few months and wouldn't be needing it for high school (our school no longer went to grade twelve). She also bought me new shoes, and I went to have my hair done every morning. I don't know where my mother found the money for all this.

At the awards presentation, my family was well represented. My parents were there, my older brother, several aunts and uncles, all beaming with pride. I still have the program for the evening, and there is a quote from Monseigneur Camille Roy on the inside page that illustrates the link that was made between the honouring of the French language and our patriotism:

> Personne n'est plus Canadien, chez nous, que nous-mêmes, qui avons les premiers occupé le pays, qui avons posé, dans le sang et les sacrifices de notre race, les fondements indestructibles de la patrie canadienne.
>
> (No one is more Canadian than we are, we who first settled this

country, who laid down, by the blood and sacrifices of our race, the indestructible foundation of the Canadian nation.)

I made the trip up to the podium five times, receiving a first prize in spelling, second prizes in improvisation, literature, composition, and handwriting. Since each prize consisted of several books, by the end of the evening I had won so many I couldn't carry them all. Although I wasn't a finalist and wouldn't be going to the next stage of the competition, my teachers made a big fuss over my prizes, which I had to display in the school lobby. I was made to feel that I had brought great honour to my school. That I had done my bit to preserve and protect the glory of the French language.

God, is it any wonder that I feel guilty reading the list of English ingredients on my cereal box in the morning?

Half a year later, I went off to high school, a French convent in downtown Ottawa. It was my first real taste of life outside the parish. Every day I got on a bus and went to school with strangers.

I didn't like the convent. It was too much like the school I had just left. Getting on the bus every morning – a new experience for me, since I had always walked to school – I expected adventure, not more of the same. My brother was going to an English Catholic high school and was quite enthusiastic about all the activities there: sports (football, hockey, basketball, volleyball) and various clubs and organizations. The convent had none of these things, not even a gym (although one was under construction).

So the next year, I followed in my brother's footsteps and went to St. Joseph's. This was not uncommon in Ontario, going to a French primary school and an English secondary school. But since French was my best subject, I had never even considered going to an English high school.

I never regretted my choice. St. Joseph's had very high academic standards and a lot of extra-curricular activities that were unheard of in French schools, mostly for lack of money. I joined the United Nations Club and the Library Club and tried out for the track team. Although I did well academically, making the honour roll by the second semester, it was a bewildering year.

First there was the adjustment to having everything taught in English instead of French. Although I was made to feel welcome by everyone, I often felt isolated, alone. My new friends were so different from my French friends, I always wondered if they really liked me.

This is what I wrote in a journal I kept for my English composition class:

> "Je me souviens." All day these words kept popping in my mind. I guess it's because of what someone said to me: Anything French, you like. Am I wrong? Do I really put too much weight on culture? I still think being French-Canadian is an honour, something I should not be ashamed of. Why do people treat us like a minority, like freaks! I came to an English school to speak and study English better. But should I forget that proud motto "Je me souviens"? I can't just let people forget we exist. We are *canadiens*, not French from France, and that's what we want people to know. Am I too idealistic to think that one day we'll understand each other? (March 15, 1966)

I did very well in this English composition class: one of my short stories appeared in the Christmas issue of a magazine published by the religious order that ran the school. I also won a city-wide slogan contest (English high school category) for Canada's centennial, which was being celebrated the following year.

The little soldier of the French language, the proud recipient of five prizes at *le Concours de français*, publishing in the language of the "enemy"? Winning an English slogan contest? Although my parents were proud, they did not brag to the rest of the family about these achievements. It would have been too hard to explain, would have upset too many people.

And they probably felt guilty for letting me go to an English high school when I was so good in French.

The following year I moved with my family to Saint-Jean-sur-Richelieu, south of Montréal, where we lived for two years. But my "emigration" had already begun, I was already on the road to becoming bicultural.

3. Rednecks in Stereo

October 1970. Now that they have found Pierre Laporte's body, it will only get worse. The nasty comments, the subtle and not-so-subtle insults. Of all the times to be living in Québec and working in Ottawa, when the country is being held to ransom by two-bit terrorists.

The last ten days have been torture. I'm the only French Canadian in the office and an easy target for the rednecks.

"Did you have to show your passport when you crossed the border this morning?"

"I thought they closed the border. Didn't they say on the news that they closed the border?"

"Are any of your PQ friends in jail yet?"

"Did you hear about that guy Laporte? Those slimy bastards killed him. Here they're holding this British guy and what do they do, they kill the Frenchie instead. Just goes to show you how stupid they are."

I try to ignore them, to do my filing and stay out of their way. I reported them to my boss the other day, but he just looked at me over his half-glasses and said: "There's a national emergency out there, Miss. They're just blowing off a little steam. Don't take it personal."

I make the mistake of leaving my purse on my desk after coffee break. When I finish my filing, I find two of them going through my purse.

"What do you think you're doing?"

They look up in mock innocence. "Didn't you read that memo from Security Services? It said to report any suspicious package or unattended parcel. We're just checking for a bomb."

"That's my purse, and you have no right to go through my things!" I try to keep the panic out of my voice. I feel like a little girl again, trying to get home but finding two bullies in the way.

"Well, lookie here," says one of the guys, holding up my birth control pills and fiddling with the plastic dial. He lets the little yellow pills drop out, one at a time. Luckily I'm at the end of my cycle and there are only a few pills left.

"I'm surprised you're even taking these. What's the matter? Don't you want to produce little terrorists?"

I try to grab the package away from him but he just holds it up in the air, out of my reach. I try to stare him down but he doesn't even blink. Although the package is now empty and I have no intention of retrieving the pills that tumbled out, I desperately want to make a stand. Knowing it will probably just make things worse.

"Give me that container or I'll report you."

"Go ahead and report me, frog fucker," he tells me, throwing the empty container in my face.

I grab the rest of my belongings and stuff them back in my purse with shaking hands. Everyone is just standing around, watching, although none of them will look me in the eye.

I'd like to say something, anything, but I don't trust my voice.

I take my coat and walk out with as much dignity as I can muster.

* * *

I NEVER REPORTED THE INCIDENT; I PRETENDED it had never happened. It would have been terribly embarrassing to explain to my supervisor what Fred had found in my purse or to repeat what he said to me. Birth control was not openly discussed in those days. The word *fuck* and its variations weren't as common as they are now, not in mixed company, at least.

Even a year later, I would have reacted differently, I would have raised more of a fuss. But I was naive and scared, unnerved by the murder of Pierre Laporte and the escalation of the crisis.

I have dealt with my share of rednecks and, because I'm bilingual, I get to listen to the ignorant comments on both sides, or rednecks in stereo. When people don't realize that you're from the "other side," they often say things in front of you that they wouldn't say otherwise.

Being French Canadian, I of course react more strongly to the anti-French remarks. I'm only human. But the attitude behind these ignorant remarks on both sides is the same. Intolerance. Lack of respect.

Here are some of the comments that have been directed at me by English and French Canadians over the years:

"What does Québec want?"

This question is used the same way as Freud's dismissive "What do women want?" – to imply that what Québec wants is unreasonable, unacceptable, or just plain contrary.

Québec has been very consistent and vocal in its demands, but so have many other provinces. It is because Québec's demands are *different* that they are singled out. Since Québec is concerned with the preservation of its language and culture, it sees control over such areas as communications and immigration (now under federal jurisdiction) as essential to its own language policies.

There is also resentment because Québec has a lot of political clout. But so does Ontario, and no one goes around saying "What does Ontario want?" in that same dismissive way.

As a strong federalist not living in Québec, I'm always in a quandary when somebody asks me what Québec wants. Sometimes I'm flippant and say, "Don't ask me. Ask Québec." Other times, I feel compelled to explain its demands and the priorities they reflect. *Explain*, not defend, since I often don't agree with them.

"Stop shoving French down our throats!"

This comment is without a doubt the most common and the most irritating I have been subjected to. I have heard it across Canada, even abroad (see chapter 8). Official bilingualism is a policy of the federal government, not of individual

French Canadians. I am not personally responsible for the Official Languages Act.

I find the comment particularly galling because I speak English and the people who tell me I'm shoving French down their throats can do so only because I understand their language. Is this why I learned English, so I can listen to people who hate the French?

I am familiar with and have great respect for the traditions, literature, and history of this country, which is more than I can say of any person who has ever made that comment to me.

I realize that many people resent official bilingualism and that the comment reflects that resentment. But I am so tired of hearing it. I am so tired of reacting to it.

"Go back to France!"

This is slowly being replaced by *"Go back to Québec!"* but the intention is the same. I've heard that more often than I can count. My ancestors, on my father's side, have been in Canada since the seventeenth century – which is considerably longer than the ancestors of most of the people who have told me to go back to France. In a country full of people who have come from somewhere else, it's amazing to me that the comment is made at all.

Canada is my home, Ottawa is my home, and I'm not going anywhere.

"The French lost on the Plains of Abraham, didn't they?"

Yes, the French lost on the Plains of Abraham, and the French went back to France. Most of the *habitants* who stayed behind on the shores of the St. Lawrence had never even been to France; they were already calling themselves *canadiens*. They had no political clout. And yet, starting with the Quebec Act of 1774, their rights and those of their descendants have been given various forms of "protection" for more than two hundred years.

The battle on the Plains of Abraham took place in 1759. Why are we still harping on who won and who lost when we're fighting another far more important battle in the late twentieth century, a battle for the survival of our country?

If Canada breaks apart, we all lose. Every single one of us.

"This is an English country, you stupid frog!"

I was singing "O Canada" in French on Parliament Hill on Canada Day when somebody objected to my choice of language. Luckily, my son was only four years old and didn't understand what was going on. Later, as we walked home, hand in hand, he asked me: "Why did that man call you a frog, Mommy? Was he just being silly?" Silly indeed!

I always sing "O Canada" in French, wherever I may be, even though I know the English lyrics. To me, singing the national anthem is a personal affirmation of my feelings for my country. My patriotism (if that word is still allowed) is intimately linked to my childhood, my French-Canadian childhood.

The song was originally written in French, and I'm sure Adolphe-Basile Routhier (who wrote the lyrics) would turn over in his grave if he knew that a French Canadian would one day be chastised for singing "O Canada" in the original French. And on Canada Day of all days.

But that was the act of one person. What about the hundreds who jeered the French words to "O Canada" at the Skydome in Toronto, before a Blue Jays game?

I don't like the monarchy, but I don't boo the Queen when she comes to Canada; I don't jeer when they play "God Save the Queen."

"You only got the job because you're bilingual."

The ultimate put-down. If you're francophone in the public service, you never get a job because of your experience, hard work, or personal suitability. You always get it because you're bilingual.

Even if the job is classified unilingual English (many editing jobs are unilingual because most people write and edit in only one language), people still think you got it because you're bilingual. It happened to me once. I wasn't looking for a unilingual English position, I was just looking for a job. I was one of ten candidates, all of whom were asked to write a test. When I was offered the job, I took it, although I knew some of the unsuccessful candidates were already working in the section.

After a few weeks, I was having lunch with my co-workers when the discussion turned to jobs. One of the unsuccessful candidates said that francophones were already hogging all the bilingual jobs and now they were coming after the unilingual ones. She was looking straight at me as she said it. I would have loved to say something nasty but I didn't want to start a feud. I couldn't very well tell her I was hired because I wrote better English than she did.

"You're so lucky to be bilingual."
This is not a bigoted comment, but it is insensitive and misleading. Many French Canadians learned English because they had to, sometimes under trying or difficult circumstances.

Learning a second language at a young age (when choice doesn't come into it) doesn't guarantee that you will retain it all your life. Most people who are bilingual have worked at staying bilingual. Because the more often you use two languages, the more you have to work at keeping them separate, otherwise one language starts to influence the other.

French Canadians in English provinces feel "lucky" to be bilingual not because they learned English but because they managed to retain their French! Often against great odds. So if you tell them they're lucky to be bilingual, they might not appreciate it.

❋ ❋ ❋

One of the drawbacks of being bilingual is being insulted

by both sides. The French-baiters get to insult me in English (and only because I understand their language) and the anti-English faction gets to attack my biculturalism, my affinity for the *maudits anglais*.

"Maudite vendue!" (Damn traitor!)

This is more than a comment. It's an accusation and a rejection. And no matter how many times I hear it, it never fails to hurt me. You wouldn't like to be called a traitor either, for living your own life, making your own choices. And when you come from a community where belonging is so important, the rejection is doubly painful.

I don't think an English Canadian who becomes bilingual, bicultural, is considered a traitor by other English Canadians. Nor will a French Canadian who becomes bilingual, as long as he or she continues to live in the French culture. But the minute you choose to be bicultural, to live in both cultures, you've sold out. The fact that you still consider yourself a French Canadian, that you live a large part of your life in French, doesn't matter. You have stepped across the great Canadian cultural divide and you have to pay the price for it.

"Your French isn't bad for an anglophone."

Learning another language takes a lot of time and effort. And to use it in public takes a certain amount of courage. So the above comment is a stupid thing to say to anyone who has learned another language. It's a double insult when the comment is being made about your mother tongue and not your second language. The man who told me this was a Québécois who assumed I was anglophone because I came from Ontario. And this is after speaking with me in French several times and knowing my very francophone name.

"That word is an anglicism. Please use the correct term."

I was making a presentation to more than two hundred people when someone from the audience interrupted to tell me I was using an anglicism. The man's interruption was inexcusable and rude. Even if I had used an English word, instead of an anglicism, it would not have been sufficient reason to embarrass me in front of everyone. To make matters worse, I found out later that the word was not an anglicism at all.

"You francos sure talk funny."

A comment I have heard far too often from my Québec cousins. There is a whole generation of Québécois who have learned a generic quasi-bureaucratic kind of French and who are quite intolerant of the dialects of their own province. Not to say downright disdainful of the poor francos who live outside their hallowed walls.

"Mêle-toi de tes maudites affaires!" (It's none of your damn business!)

I once tried to help a bewildered tourist in Quebec City who couldn't understand what a salesclerk was saying. I knew from the look on the clerk's face that she understood English but didn't want to speak it. When the tourist left, apologizing profusely to the girl for inconveniencing her, I told the clerk she should be ashamed of herself. She looked me right in the eye and called me an *anglo bitch*.

* * *

Since I'm not an English Canadian, I don't get called names that are reserved for them, but I hear them often enough:

"Maudits anglais!" is pretty universal. There are equivalents for every nationality, race, or religion. "Damn (insert relevant label)!" It is used randomly and often.

"Têtes carrées." (Square heads, roughly equivalent to blockheads.) Like all such terms, it presumes certain characteristics about people just because they're English.

"C'est rien que la piastre qui compte!" I don't know how prevalent this is now but it was common when I was younger. It paints the English as money-grabbers, for whom only the buck counts.

Sometimes, however, there is no redneck comment, no ugly generalization, just a lack of awareness. Once when some friends of mine came to Ottawa for the weekend, I took them to Parliament Hill to see the light and sound show. Having never been to the show, I didn't realize that there were separate presentations in French and in English. We arrived in the middle of the French one.

My friends were from southern Ontario and not used to encountering much French. They continued talking, although there were people all around us who were trying to listen. I tried to shush them, but they kept on chatting. Because they didn't understand French, they didn't hear it and were oblivious to the fact that others were trying to listen.

Because I work for the federal government, I often attend annual meetings of national organizations and their closing banquets. The two solitudes are never more evident than at such occasions. The Québécois sit at their tables and the English at theirs.

I remember one particular banquet in Toronto. Although almost half the membership of this particular organization was from Québec, the program for the evening was entirely in English: the speeches as well as the entertainment. It didn't take long for the French Canadians to start talking and ignoring what was going on at the head table. At first I was ashamed because they were being rude. But as the evening progressed, I was also angry at the organizers for planning an all-English program. At the banquet in Quebec City the previous year, the program had been bilingual.

At a track-and-field event in Ottawa, someone asked me what the announcer was saying. I translated automatically, thinking the man had missed the English announcement that came first. "No," he said, "what language is he speaking?" I just stared at the man. I couldn't believe that someone who had lived his whole life in Ottawa (he told me this earlier) wasn't able to even recognize French (not understand, just recognize) when he heard it. What language did he think the announcer was using, Swahili?

But these individual comments and incidents pale in comparison to the frenzy of intolerance that greeted the Meech Lake Accord, Bill 178 in Québec, and Bill 8 in Ontario.

The frenzy was perhaps an illusion, brought on by the media's obsession with English-French tensions. Or perhaps these kinds of incidents happen all the time but never get reported.

Thanks to television, I now have witnessed the expression of more anti-French sentiment in one year than I have in my own lifetime. Camera crews have brought me into the council chambers of Ontario municipalities to listen to their declarations of unilingualism. They have brought me the rantings of a man who believes that bilingualism is like the AIDS virus, and of an organization that encourages people to wipe their feet on a Québec flag.

There was such contempt in that gesture, from a generation that supposedly respects symbols such as flags. It's one thing to see rebellious teenagers burn a flag in protest, quite another to see grey-haired seniors, who have lived through a world war, show such disrespect.

The camera crews were also on the look-out for anti-English sentiment. They brought me marches in support of Bill 178, zeroing in on the more offensive placards, showing us the burning of a Canadian flag. They showed me students fighting each other over the use of English in the hallways and schoolyard of a French school in Montréal. They took me to Hull where the youth wing of the Parti Québécois was out hunting for English commercial signs. They brought me the mayor congratulating them for taking pride in their language. Applauded for spying on their fellow citizens. Shades of Big Brother. Or should I say *Grand Frère*.

Rednecks inadvertently became stars on the national news. Their every word and gesture was documented and disseminated throughout the land.

Just what we needed. More intolerance. More ignorant comments about the French and the English. I watched the coverage with a sinking heart. *Plus ça change, plus c'est la même chose.* The more it changes, the more it remains the same.

Just as violence begets violence, bigotry begets bigotry. And I have to listen to it all in stereo.

4. Bits and Pieces of the Past

The Eastern Townships in the fall. Driving down a road that is framed by yellow light, the birch tree leaves radiating colour as wood in a fireplace radiates heat.

Always partial to yellow, I am delighted by the delicious excess of it.

Eventually, the yellowness starts to recede. Although birches are still lining the road, they are without leaf, without life. Pretty soon there are no trees.

"We must be approaching the town," my husband says.

The town we are approaching is Asbestos, Québec. Not your everyday kind of destination. A town that became famous in 1949, when some miners stood up to the Johns-Manville Corporation and the Duplessis government. When some prominent members of the Catholic church hierarchy sided with the strikers.

The town's short-lived fame was rekindled years later when some of the players surfaced on the federal scene in Ottawa in the late sixties. Jean Marchand was a union organizer, Gérard Pelletier covered the strike for *Le Devoir*. Pierre Elliott Trudeau, who would one day become prime minister and appoint these two men to his cabinet, also spent several weeks in Asbestos during the strike.

Chance has brought me here. My husband had some business with the Johns-Manville Corporation and I asked to tag along. He didn't understand why I would want to come here. I'm not sure I know why either. I leave him at the company office and wander off on my own.

So this is Asbestos. I didn't expect it to be so ugly. But then, what do I know about mining towns? Perhaps it's just the contrast after driving through that spectacular foliage.

I stand well away from the edge of the open pit that threatens to swallow up the town. I just never expected the mine to be right there, in the middle of everything, where the town square should be. Like a gaping wound, spreading every year, claiming another street, another row of houses.

I've been to many "official" historic sites – Louisbourg, Annapolis Royal, the Plains of Abraham – but they didn't move me. Asbestos does. I look for a plaque, some kind of testimonial to what happened here. I do not find one.

Tales of the strike were a part of my childhood; there were a lot of union men living on my street, mostly railway workers. One of our neighbours was distantly related to Monseigneur Charbonneau, the archbishop of Montréal, who sided openly with the strikers and was "exiled" to Vancouver for his pains. When he died his body was returned to Montréal, and there were throngs of people to welcome the exile home.

Some say the Asbestos strike presaged the Quiet Revolution. That it was the first symbolic break with the past. But I wonder. Does a conquered people ever really break with the past?

* * *

I DON'T KNOW IF HISTORY REPEATS ITSELF BUT the history of a conquered people repeats itself *ad nauseam*.

First there is the act of conquest. The event that bisects the history of a conquered people into the glorious "before" and the terrible "after". Then there are the many small defeats that remind people of their great loss, of their continued disgrace. French Canadians are raised on this kind of history.

Contrast this with the history of the British Empire, a history of conquest too, but of conquerors not the conquered. A history of power, wealth, and influence.

Or with the history of Canada (as seen by English Canadians), a history of slow steady progress from colony to nation – as the eldest daughter of the Empire, then the Commonwealth – its emergence as a peace broker on the world scene. A history of evolution, not revolution.

Or with the history of our American neighbours, who went from colonial to superpower status in less than two hundred years. A history of manifest destiny.

I don't want to talk about the history that is actually taught in our schools or the ground-breaking research undertaken by our historians, but what we tend to remember about the past. The bits and pieces that we carry around in our heads and in our hearts. That are embedded in our culture.

Our past is not a neat package but a jumble of dates, events, places, and people. We can find bits and pieces of Canada's past in our monuments, traditions, ceremonies, and special holidays. We have woven them into legends, poems, stories, and songs. These bits and pieces are deeply rooted, emotionally charged, and immune to historical revision. Every nation has them, every culture.

History is a nation's childhood memories. Just as what we remember about our childhood says more about what we've become than what actually happened to us, what we remember about our history says more about the kind of nation we've become than what actually happened in the past. Only our childhood memories are not the same. Québec's memories are of an abused childhood, with Britain and then English Canada as the abusers.

Canada has not one history but many histories, some of which have been ignored, some of which have been over-emphasized. By continuing to foster the two-founding-nations myth, we perpetuate a history that excludes more Canadians than it includes.

I know that history textbooks have changed radically since I went to school, that they now acknowledge our Native peoples and the role of immigrants in the building of this country, and that they highlight Canada's social evolution as well as its political development. But our continued obsession with linguistic duality undermines the way we look at the past, which in turn undermines the way we look at the future.

Let me share with you the bits and pieces of my people's past, bits and pieces that have survived in my mind and heart, in spite of two university degrees in history.

I'm not obsessed by the Conquest. It happened, I can't do anything to change it. But I do understand how it has shaped the history of my people into a catalogue of its many struggles to stay alive, to preserve its identity.

Although I went to school in Ontario, the history I remember is very different from the history English Ontarians remember. Instead of the arrival of the Loyalists, the Family Compact, clergy reserves, the War of 1812, William Lyon Mackenzie, the Fathers of Confederation, the building of the Canadian Pacific Railway, the settlement of the West, the Boer War, the Winnipeg Strike, the Depression, and the two world wars, I remember Samuel de Champlain, the seigneurial system, Jean Talon, the Acadian Deportation, the Plains of Abraham, Louis-Joseph Papineau, Lord Durham's report, the hanging of Louis Riel, the Manitoba Schools Question, Regulation 17, the conscription crisis, and the Asbestos strike.

First, the glorious "before," the history of New France.

Jacques Cartier and 1534 are the first two facts I remember. Where exactly Cartier landed or how many boats he had may or may not have been part of the lesson. But in my mind, I can still see the large cross with three *fleurs-de-lis* and a little scroll that read *le Roy de France*. A cross he supposedly erected to claim the land for France. There must have been a picture or drawing in my history book, since I can visualize it so clearly.

Samuel de Champlain is the next heroic figure, the founding of Québec in 1608 the next memorable date.

The various expeditions of the Recollets and later the Jesuits were explained in great detail, but the Indians they were trying to convert were mentioned only in passing. The role of Indians in opening up the fur trade was more than eclipsed by the tales of their "barbaric" torture of missionaries.

There wasn't that much emphasis on the fur trade, the focus being more on the growing settlement of New France. We learned about Louis Hébert, his wife, and their three children, the "first" farming family of New France. The founding of Montréal by de Maisonneuve in 1642. The bravery of Dollard des Ormeaux who died with all his men trying to defend Montréal (I found out later that he was attacked because he was trying to seize furs directly from the Iroquois).

We learned about *les filles du roi*, the young girls who came from France to marry the many single settlers in the new colony. Some had royal dowries, hence the term *the King's daughters*. I used to imagine how brave they were to leave their families and friends, to marry strangers in the wilds of New France. I had no way of knowing that many of these girls were orphaned or without means of support. That a marriage arranged by the state, even if it were in the wilds of New France, might have seemed a less scary alternative than a life of destitution.

I had visions of *seigneuries*, long and narrow, along the beautiful St. Lawrence, the stately *manoir du seigneur*, the modest church, the neat habitations of the *censitaires*. I don't know if this idyllic view of the seigneurial system was learned or imagined.

We learned about the various intendants, about the able management of Jean Talon who conducted the first census of the colony and the corruption of the last intendant, François Bigot.

The *coureurs de bois* and the *voyageurs* were mentioned only in passing. Perhaps the nuns thought they were too disreputable. We did not dwell on the adventures of des Groseilliers and Radisson, Jolliet and Marquette, La Salle, or La Vérendrye, although their exploits were praised for extending the frontiers of France's territory in North America.

The importance of religion in the colony was of course well documented. We read excerpts from the *Relations des jésuites*, recounted the martyrdom of de Brébeuf and Lalemant and their fellow missionaries, extolled the good deeds of the Ursulines in Québec and Montréal; there was plenty of material to inspire admiration among impressionable Catholic girls.

And there were many heroines for us to admire: Jeanne Mance who founded and ran a hospital in the struggling new settlement of Montréal. Marguerite Bourgeoys who founded the first Canadian order, the Congrégation de Notre-Dame de Montréal, dedicated to the teaching of young girls. Madeleine de Verchères who helped to defend her family's *seigneurie* from the Iroquois until reinforcements could come from Montréal.

This is the history the good nuns taught me. The emphasis was on the glory of France and of the Catholic church. Then the glory ended and the terrible "after" began. Although the Conquest marks the official beginning of the terrible "after," it actually started with the Acadian Deportation.

Most Canadians think the Deportation had an impact only on the Acadians and their descendants. But the long-lasting legacy of that cruel decision has been to colour the way most French Canadians (not just Acadians) view the English, even though the same fate did not await the *canadiens* on the shores of the St. Lawrence. The Deportation was what the "big bad" English were capable of. (Never mind the way the French treated Indians. I was not aware of such contradictions then.)

The Deportation was the first in a long series of "wrongs" done to my people. The history I was taught from that moment on focused on these wrongs. It did not celebrate achievements. Our only achievement was survival.

As in any history of a conquered people, the critical event was the great catastrophe, the Conquest. Although the capitulation of New France didn't happen for another year, the Conquest is most identified with the battle of the Plains of Abraham on September 13, 1759, a battle that apparently lasted only fifteen minutes.

Fifteen minutes that changed things forever.

The Conquest is the "big bang" of our history, hurling fragments of the past into the orbit of the future, and forever altering the chronicling of that past. From tales of glory to *la survivance*, from physical survival in the wilderness to cultural survival under the British.

I was taught to be grateful for the Quebec Act of 1774, which recognized Roman Catholicism, the seigneurial system, and the French civil code. To welcome the creation of Upper and Lower Canada in 1791, which gave French Canada a territory all its own. The War of 1812 was barely mentioned. We spent considerable time on the *patriotes* and their leader, Louis-Joseph Papineau, and on the rebellions in Lower Canada in 1837. William Lyon Mackenzie and the rebellion in Upper Canada were more or less ignored.

We dwelled on the Durham Report and its stated intention of assimilating the French. Lord Durham's indictment of French Canada as "an old and stationary society, in a new and progressive world" was much quoted, along with his famous description of Upper and Lower Canada as "two nations warring in the bosom of a single state."

Confederation and the British North America Act of 1867 were not given great prominence. They were neither praised nor condemned. Confederation was sort of glossed over, not identified as the birth of Canada. I remember being surprised in 1967 with the fuss over the centennial. Since I thought Canada was more than three hundred years old, a centennial seemed a strange anniversary to be celebrating.

I don't remember exactly what I was taught about Louis Riel, only that his hanging inspired the same aversion the Acadian Deportation did. It was another example of what the "cruel" English could do – hang an innocent man who was fighting for a desperate cause. When I was in Winnipeg several years ago, standing in front of Riel's commemorative statue, an older man came up to me and said: "You know, if that guy hadn't had French blood in him, you never would have heard of him. And his statue wouldn't be standing here in this park."

In the history I was taught as a girl, Manitoba figured twice, in the Riel Rebellion and the Manitoba Schools Question.

Although the issue was about separate schools (Manitoba wanted to abolish them), I remember it as a language question. Perhaps because separate schools in my mind were always French schools. In any event, the issue was given prominence as an example of what happened to minority rights in the rest of Canada.

French Canada's objection to participating in Britain's wars was another big theme. First, the Boer War in 1899, in which Canada participated against the wishes of Québec (although the regiments were made up of volunteers); but more particularly, the two world wars and the conscription crises they precipitated.

In Ontario, we didn't have a deportation to deplore, or a Louis Riel to mourn, but we had Regulation 17. When I was very little and heard adults discussing *le règlement 17* in hushed tones, I always wondered what they were talking about. For years, it was a mystery to me. At one point, I became convinced it was a combination of the Ten Commandments and the seven cardinal sins (the only two religious numbers I knew that added up to seventeen).

A history lesson eventually cleared up the mystery. Regulation 17 was the culmination of a gradual restriction of French as a language of instruction in Ontario schools, a process that had started as early as 1885, the year Riel was hanged. Passed in 1912, this regulation limited the use of French in schools to the first two years. There was much conflict and bitterness over this regulation, and an Ottawa school board even closed its schools over the matter. But the regulation, which was amended in 1927 to allow teaching in French where the numbers warranted, remained on the books until 1947.

Not as earthshaking as the deportation of a people or the hanging of a hero, but it was a tragedy unique to French Ontario. "Souvenez-vous du règlement dix-sept" we were told as children. "Souvenez-vous toujours du règlement dix-sept."

This is the history I was taught as a child, a mixture of

emotion and fact. It greatly influenced my sense of self, my sense of identity as a French Canadian. Although the emphasis may have changed, certainly the references to the religious aspects, I would venture to guess that the history taught in Québec primary schools today has many of the same elements I remember.

At university, I discovered a new kind of history, scientific and objective. We spent a lot of time demolishing historical myths, disproving schools of interpretation. The more I read and studied, the more I questioned the interpretations, the more enamoured with the "objectivity" of history I became. I never admitted to my professors what a struggle I had with the bits and pieces of the past that were in my head and heart. They surfaced at the most inopportune moments, sometimes inaccurate, even irrational, but very much intact. They created a tremendous bias that I constantly had to overcome.

As much as I would have liked to study for a Ph.D. in history, personal circumstances forced me back into the real world. With each passing year, the possibilities of working in my chosen field dimmed. I earned my living as a writer and researcher but not as a historian. The only contact I now have with history are the books I read.

My experience as a graduate student convinced me of the inherent subjectivity of history, a subjectivity I had experienced first hand as the descendant of a conquered people. Academic objectivity was no match for the bits and pieces of my past.

The issue of funding for Catholic schools in Ontario made me realize how these bits and pieces could short-circuit both my scholarly training and my political convictions.

I am not a practising Catholic. My son is not baptized, and he goes to a French public school. Yet when the Ontario government decided to extend funding to the last three years of Catholic high school (grades eleven, twelve, and thirteen), I "sided" with the Catholics.

Although I had personally rejected the separate school system for my own child, I believed separate schools were entitled to receive funding for all grades, just like the public schools. Raised as a Catholic myself, I had no trouble understanding why Catholics wanted to maintain a separate school system, why they believed religion was an integral part of education. Separation of church and state (in this case, keeping religion out of state-controlled schools) is a Protestant concept, not a Catholic one.

And yet, I shared the concern of other parents who believed that separate school systems are expensive and create unnecessary duplication. I also recognized that those of other faiths who believed religion was an integral part of education had to organize private schools that received no government funding. But the bits and pieces of my past, the fact that my mother had to pay to send us to Catholic high schools, that all French schools in Ontario were separate schools (which is no longer the case), won in the end and I supported the extended funding.

We can't change the bits and pieces of the past that we carry in our hearts and in our heads. They can't be "rewritten" the way a history text can be rewritten to reflect new research, new evidence, new interpretations. But we must be conscious of them in order to understand how they affect us, how they shape our opinions and decisions, political and otherwise.

We also have to realize that, as Canadians, we do not share the same bits and pieces of the past. And yet we are trying to build our future on these fragments, to enshrine them in our constitution.

Much has been said about the importance of history, of knowing the past. That those who cannot remember the past are condemned to repeat it (George Santayana). That the farther backward we can look, the farther forward we can see (Winston Churchill). I prefer what Ludwig Wittgenstein had to say about the present, that if we live in the present, we live in eternity. Since we cannot share the same past, let us at least live in the same present and work towards the same future.

We have to let go of the past – but in so doing, there is a danger. That Québec may let go of Canada, may consider the last 123 years as a period of occupation. Québec might start afresh, with a new past and a new future – and forever change the past and the future of Canada.

5. Separation Anxiety

Tuesday, May 20, 1980, the day of the referendum on sovereignty-association. Without a doubt, the most agonizing day of my double life.

I'm waiting for the results of the vote in the privacy of my living-room, although I've been invited to a number of "victory" parties. Since I have family and friends in both camps, I didn't want to choose sides, even to watch the results on television. So I sit at home, isolated in my ambivalence.

I'm in no hurry for the final tally. If they voted yes, my world will change forever. If they voted no, I'll have to wait a while longer for the forever part. Because even if the referendum is lost, it won't be the end of sovereignty-association. Time and changing demographics will see to that.

When the results are finally announced, the gap is wider than I expected, roughly 60 per cent against, 40 per cent for. I feel no elation because the *no* vote prevailed. Only a mixture of relief and sadness. An overwhelming sadness because the *yes* vote meant so much to some of my friends, to a whole generation, my generation.

I suffer through the television coverage, not to watch Claude Ryan claiming victory, not to listen to Trudeau, Chrétien, and Lalonde, but to see and hear René Lévesque. I may be at home but my heart is in the Paul-Sauvé Arena.

When René finally appears on stage, disappointed but defiant, I stand up with the rest of them. I feel foolish, but I don't sit down again.

Every time he tries to speak, he is drowned out by the crowd. So he shrugs and waits, tears in his eyes. When there is finally a lull, he says simply: "Si je vous entends bien, vous êtes en train de dire: à la prochaine fois." (If I hear you correctly, you are telling me: until the next time.)

The crowd agrees with him, the people clapping rhythmically, whistling, and chanting "René! René!" He starts them on the lyrics to Québec's unofficial anthem: "Gens du pays, c'est votre tour, de vous laisser parler d'amour…"

I try to sing with them, but my voice keeps breaking. As I watch them hug each other, openly weeping, mourning their loss, I also feel a terrible sense of loss. They're sad because their dream didn't come true. I'm sad because they had the dream in the first place. Because my dream of a nation is not limited to the borders of Québec.

I'm crying because it always comes to this. My two worlds rejecting each other. The relief and the sadness I felt only a short while ago seem inadequate and paltry emotions considering the magnitude of what has just been decided. How many nations ever choose to be born? Ever start from scratch? Québec isn't saying yes to Canada but no to itself.

I feel as if I'm in the middle of an earthquake. The earth is splitting beneath my feet, and I can't decide which side to jump to. Falling in the chasm somehow seems an easier choice.

✽ ✽ ✽

I SHOULD HAVE BEEN USED TO IT. THE EARTH-quake scenario, I mean. My two worlds, the one in which I was born and the one in which I live, have been rejecting each other all my adult life.

The FLQ Crisis in October 1970 was the first tremor that shook my little world. And shook it hard. The fact that I was living in Québec at the time and working in Ottawa added an extra twist to the events of those fateful days.

I was living in Hull because rents were cheaper, not because I wanted to live in the "mother province" as some of my friends did.

Mouthy and opinionated, like many twenty-year-olds, I was left of the political spectrum but hardly a radical. Six months earlier, even though I couldn't vote (I was a month short of twenty, the voting age at the time), I had taken an active interest in the Québec elections. The elections in which the Parti Québécois fielded its first candidates.

Although I didn't join the party, I was interested in the socialist elements of its platform and would have voted for the PQ candidate if I had been of age. So when a friend asked me to distribute some PQ campaign literature in a couple of apartment buildings, I readily agreed. I got a PQ button for my efforts and wore it to work until the day of the elections, although I knew that as a civil servant I was supposed to be neutral.

When James Cross, and later Pierre Laporte, were kidnapped by the FLQ, my link to the Parti Québécois, however marginal, was fresh in the minds of my co-workers. My big mouth, the fact that I lived in Québec, and my now infamous Parti Québécois campaign button guaranteed that I would be hassled and I was. Culminating in the "frog fucker" incident.

The night Pierre Laporte's body was found, we were having a small dinner party. There were four of us, two French-Canadian women and our European husbands. We talked about the crisis and about the change in our co-workers, who no longer saw us as individuals but as strangers, suspicious strangers. My friend's husband, who was Hungarian, talked about his experiences during the 1956 uprising and how he had fled his home country. We were all pretty gloomy by the time the evening ended.

The radio confirmed our gloom with news that Pierre Laporte's body had been found. Our friends had already left, but we called them to share the terrible news.

I never thought the kidnappers would actually kill one of the hostages. I was outraged and ashamed. Outraged that they had killed an innocent man, ashamed that they were French Canadian like me. I had never heard of Pierre Laporte but I cried for him, for us, for all of us.

In the sixties, there had been major riots and several assassinations south of the border, bloody demonstrations and acts of terrorism in Europe. Canada had escaped relatively unscathed, a few bombs in a few mailboxes. But now with this act of murder, we were being welcomed into the real world where hijackings, kidnappings, executions, and other acts of terrorism were the ultimate political statements.

This was an act of terrorism in Canada, committed in the name of freedom for my people. It made me feel guilty and ashamed that I had not taken it seriously, that I had ranted and raved about the government's "overreaction." I didn't change my mind about the imposition of the War Measures Act, but I stopped being so self-righteous about it. Self-righteousness is little consolation when you watch the body of a politician being lifted out of a car trunk on the television news.

The FLQ Crisis – or the October Crisis, as it came to be called – was my baptism of fire. The first time my vague notions of civil liberties were put to the test. I was against the invocation of the War Measures Act, but I didn't join a demonstration against it on Parliament Hill, a demonstration that was noisier than it was large, since most Canadians supported the prime minister's stand.

I didn't realize then that I would soon have a ringside seat, that I would witness one of the many actions authorized by that legislation. I was having lunch with Paulette, the friend who had asked me to help with the flyers, when two officers from the Québec Provincial Police came to search her apartment. They apologized for disturbing our meal and started to look through Paulette's books and papers, careful not to topple anything over. They did make a mess, but in the same way a customs agent makes a mess of your suitcase when you get stopped at the border. After asking Paulette a few questions, they left.

We were outraged by the incident, and that outrage dictated the way we described it. We exaggerated, told everyone that the police had ransacked the place and accused us of being communists. It wasn't our fault we got such polite policemen, that they didn't ransack the apartment as we expected them to. We knew others whose places had been torn apart.

My outrage was my way of making the crisis real. Of measuring its impact on my own life. Of protesting the way the crisis was being handled by the government. The very fact that Paulette's apartment was searched, no matter how politely, was an infringement of her civil liberties. She had done nothing except work for a legitimate political party, the PQ, in the last election. I don't know why that infringement wasn't enough, why I had to dramatize the incident to make it valid. Maybe it was to excuse my passivity, my silence in their presence.

The FLQ Crisis forced me come to grips with separatism for the first time. I had never given much thought to independence. I was not Québécoise and I was living in Québec only temporarily. I supported the Parti Québécois in spite of its goal of independence, not because of it.

Those weeks in late 1970 are as close as I ever came to becoming a separatist. I was young, living in Québec; I knew people who had been questioned by the police. But it was more than that. I was suddenly on the "other side," shoved there by people who didn't know my views on anything, let alone the FLQ or Québec independence. At first, I thought I was being hassled because of that PQ button I had worn to work in the spring. But I soon realized it went deeper than that.

It didn't matter that I was not a separatist. That I hated violence. That I rejected terrorism in all its forms. I was a French Canadian and therefore one of "them." Someone who wanted to bring down the government, bomb mail-boxes, kidnap diplomats, and execute politicians.

I couldn't believe this was all happening in Canada. The police searching apartments, making arrests, holding people without charging them. Soldiers guarding our cabinet ministers. Talk of civil war.

I couldn't believe that anyone would think I had anything to do with it.

The discovery of Pierre Laporte's body only made things

worse for me personally. As FLQ = PQ was scrawled onto walls and flashed on the television screen, I became more than a suspicious stranger, I became a potential enemy. Someone who could breed little terrorists.

The FLQ Crisis taught me an important lesson – that, under certain circumstances, just being a French Canadian could make me a threat to other Canadians. That my ethnic origin could link me to horrid crimes like bombings, kidnappings, and murder.

I was living in Ontario again when the Parti Québécois won their first election in Québec in 1976. The night of the election, I was at the National Arts Centre watching a French play, I can't remember which one, and one of the actors made a comment to the audience that he would perhaps need a passport to get back into Québec. I laughed with the others, but there was a chill in my heart. Part of me wanted the Parti Québécois to win because I still believed in its platform and I was very fond of René Lévesque. The other part of me was scared of the consequences of such a win. Scared that it would make separation inevitable.

When my husband and I got home, my brother was watching the victory speech of René Lévesque. We had just become parents two weeks before, and the play had been our first outing, my brother our first baby-sitter. I took my son, who was sleeping in my brother's arms, and held him close to me as I listened to Lévesque's speech. What would all this mean to his future? To the Canada he would know? The FLQ Crisis suddenly seemed far away. The Parti Québécois was a legitimate party, legitimately elected by the people of Québec. The win left me strangely complacent, the concern of a few hours earlier already forgotten.

But the referendum on sovereignty-association and the campaign that preceded it smashed that complacency and reopened all the wounds of the October Crisis. It was a different type of crisis. I felt left out. Helpless. What could I do? I didn't live in Québec, I had no vote, no say in the decision. Even though it would affect me for the rest of my life.

The referendum debate made me schizophrenic. I wanted Québec to stay in Canada, but I understood all too well its desire to leave. My friends from Québec tried to involve me in heated debates, to convince me to join one side or the other. I couldn't share my doubts with them, my ambivalence. By not disagreeing, by not arguing, I let friends from both sides believe that I was on their side. I might as well have lied, it would have been more honest.

I envied their certainty, their commitment, berating myself for my uncertainty, my lack of commitment. The more I tried to choose sides, the less I was able to choose.

But the debate wasn't just with my friends from Québec. I lived in an English province, one that wasn't too sympathetic to Québec's right to decide. Once again, some English Canadians assumed that they knew where I stood on the issue just because I was a French Canadian. Only this time the comments were harsher.

"I guess you'll be moving back to Québec. Too bad you can't move all the way back to France. We should have shipped you Frenchies out years ago."

I was also harsher, no longer blinded by silly tears.

"I'm not moving anywhere. This is my home. I was born here, so were my parents and my grandparents. Can you say the same? How far back does your claim go?"

People discussed the possibility of civil war, as they had done in 1970. Asked me, derisively, on which side I would fight when the time came. That question angered me more than any other. How glibly they talked about civil war, about pitting Canadian against Canadian, family against family, friend against friend! And in my case, me against myself.

The day after the referendum I was interviewing Dr. Séraphin Marion, an eminent Franco-Ontarian writer and historian. Although he was cautiously optimistic about the results, he was less optimistic about the long term.

Listening to this man, who still remembered Regulation 17, who had taught and written in French in Ontario all his life, who had devoted himself to the survival of French in the province, I felt less alone, less divided. He was eighty-four and I was thirty, but there was no generation gap between us. We shared the same ambivalence, the same sadness, the same cautious hope for the future.

Separatism is something all French Canadians have to face, sooner or later. For some of us, the decision for or against separatism is a decision we make only once. But for many of us, it's a decision we make and remake, as the political climate changes and it becomes more or less of a possibility. A reaction to events like the October Crisis, to debates generated by the referendum, the election of the Parti Québécois, the Meech Lake Accord.

The decision is obviously different for a French Canadian who doesn't live in Québec than it is for one who does. But all French Canadians will have to choose, sooner or later. If Québec separates from Canada, it will forever change the life of French Canadians in the rest of the country. They will have to decide whether to stay or to emigrate to Québec. They will be forced to make an impossible choice between the two sides of their hyphenated identity: the French part and the Canadian part.

I have many different feelings about separation: as an individual, as a Canadian, and as a believer in self-determination.

My feelings as an individual are, of course, selfish. I don't want Québec to leave, because it would forever change my world and my place within it. Separation would cause all kinds of economic, political, and personal disruptions, and those who would pay the heaviest price, emotionally and later politically, would be the French minorities in the rest of the country.

We already get dragged into every discussion about what

is going on in Québec, so can you imagine what would happen
if Québec separated? Who would there be left to blame but us,
the unassimilated remnants? We are already held responsible
for the Official Languages Act, Québec's Bill 178, Ontario's Bill
8, the Meech Lake Accord, and every Supreme Court decision
upholding minority rights.

How many insults would we have to endure because of
our French names and froggy accents? Although insults would
be the least of our worries. Our rights, as few as they are, would
quickly disappear. There would be overt discrimination, calls for
us to "go back where we came from"; only now they wouldn't
mean France but Québec, not the old country but the new
upstart one. In the minds of many, we would be "enemy aliens."

These selfish considerations aside, I have other reservations about Québec's departure. As a Canadian, I can't even
conceive of a Canada without Québec. I think the French fact
is an integral component of our Canadian identity, that Québec
is one of the linchpins of Canadian nationalism.

The irony is that the reverse isn't true. Canada is not a
linchpin of Québec nationalism. Far from it. Québec nationalism, by its very nature, excludes the rest of Canada.

We can't expect Québec to stay in Canada just to ensure
the survival of our identity or our nationalism. Québec has a
right to exist for Québec.

As much as I would hate to see Québec separate from
Canada, I believe it's the people of Québec who have to make
the choice. Although the decision would affect the rest of the
country, it is up to the people of Québec to make it. For a
French Canadian like me, it is an impossible choice. I can't
conceive of a Canada without Québec, a Québec without
Canada. For many Québécois and Québécoises, there is no
choice to be made, a Québec without Canada is already a
reality.

6. Swimming in Meech Lake

April 1988. The banquet of an annual meeting, held in a Toronto hotel. A table bringing together a mixture of business and government people from Toronto, Ottawa, and Montréal. The subject turns to federal politics and the Meech Lake Accord.

I haven't paid much attention to the accord since Trudeau appeared before a Senate committee last month. I have no strong feelings about the agreement, although I'm being told that it sets dangerous precedents.

"I think Trudeau is right. The Meech Lake Accord is fundamentally flawed and needs to be renegotiated," argues Robert, who is very involved in politics.

"Renegotiated? No way. If you reject Meech Lake, you reject Québec. Pure and simple," counters André, one of two Québécois at the table.

"My friends in Québec called the Meech Lake Accord a sell-out by Bourassa," I interject, surprised by André's vehemence.

"That's because they thought Bourassa didn't go far enough. Don't you worry, if Canada rejects Meech, they won't be singing the same tune."

"What's the Meech Lake Accord?" one of the Toronto women asks. André looks at her with a mixture of amazement and disgust but refrains from saying anything nasty.

Robert rolls his eyes at me. We've both known Marjorie for years. She is intelligent and successful but has very few interests outside her career, outside Toronto, which she thinks is the centre of the world. She has always been apolitical, not well versed in the major issues of the day.

"It's an agreement reached by the ten provincial premiers and the prime minister to include Québec in the constitution," I explain quickly, to cover the awkward silence that has developed.

"Québec isn't part of the constitution?" Marjorie continues naively.

André doesn't try to hide his exasperation. "Where the

hell were you in 1982? How can you not know that Québec, which represents a quarter of Canada's population, did not sign the constitution!"

"That's not really fair, André. If you put that question to most Canadians, they wouldn't know the answer."

"Well, in Québec, they certainly do. And the indifference of the rest of Canada is hard to take."

Marjorie is ripping her bun into little shreds. She is visibly embarrassed.

"But André," I ask, "are you seriously telling me that if I reject Meech, I'm rejecting Québec?"

"Ben oui, j'suis serieux, qu'est-ce que tu penses?" he answers impatiently in French. (Of course I'm serious, what do you think?)

"But the Meech Lake Accord isn't just about the distinct society, which I have no objection to. What bothers me is the fundamental shift in the division of powers from the federal level to the provinces," Robert argues. Robert is originally from Montréal. His mother was English, his father French. He's been a strong Liberal for years, one of the most political men I know.

"The Meech Lake Accord was drafted to bring Québec into the constitution. What you're worried about was negotiated not just by Québec but by the other provinces. So don't blame us if Brian was willing to give away the store."

The argument goes back and forth for a while longer. When I excuse myself to go to the ladies' room, Marjorie follows me. As she uncaps her lipstick, she meets my eyes in the mirror and shrugs.

"People from Québec can sure make a big fuss over nothing."

"Nothing? Didn't you see how passionately André feels about this issue? How can you call what he feels, what his fellow Quebeckers feel, nothing? Of course he's making a fuss. He's fighting for what matters most to him. His rights as a Canadian, as a Canadian who speaks French. Rights he feels were earned a long time ago – " I stop myself, surprised by the vehemence of my diatribe.

Marjorie is staring at me. I pretend to wash my hands.

"You know Marjorie," I start again, in a calmer voice. "I haven't been paying much attention to this Meech Lake Accord. But if André is right, it has just been upgraded from a constitutional compromise to a vote for Québec. And God help us if it has."

Marjorie returns the lipstick to her purse and leaves without a word.

* * *

THIS CONVERSATION TOOK PLACE IN APRIL 1988, long before the debate over the Meech Lake Accord became so bitter, more than two years before the accord sputtered and died.

Meech Lake. Only in Canada would we have a constitutional crisis named after a lake. My parish used to organize excursions to Meach Lake (as it was spelled then) when I was a child. I also went swimming there in the seventies when pollution closed the beaches on the Ottawa and Rideau rivers. I've even been in the room where the Meech Lake Accord was signed because Willson House is also used by the Privy Council Office for briefings and conferences.

How I wish Meech was still spelled Meach. And Meech Lake just a place where I used to go swimming. Instead of being linked to constitutional negotiations during the course of which every province grabbed what it could in exchange for a few words declaring Québec a distinct society. An accord that was supposed to reverse the betrayal in 1982 when the prime minister and nine provincial premiers endorsed a Canadian constitution without Québec.

Ten years after the referendum, twenty years after the FLQ

Crisis, we just had to embroil ourselves in another do-or-die debate about Canada's duality, an almost ritual rejection of each other's view of the country.

A debate that has left me feeling bruised, confused, and abused. My duality as precarious as the country's.

My opinion on the Meech Lake Accord has gone from indifference to opposition to reluctant acceptance. I was indifferent, or not paying attention, when the accord was first signed in 1987. Pierre Trudeau's appearance before a Senate committee in March 1988 to argue against the accord aroused my interest but not my concern. It was that conversation in a Toronto hotel that sounded the first alarm bells in my mind. If Meech was going to be a vote for or against Québec, then the stakes were much higher than I had realized.

As a strong federalist, I objected to the increased powers that were being given to the provinces. I was also swayed by arguments that the rights of women and Native peoples might be threatened. But as a Canadian, and a French-speaking one at that, I wanted a constitution that no longer excluded Québec. So I found myself on both sides of the debate, once again.

As the debate over Meech became less and less constitutional and more and more anti-French, I found it hard to stay on both sides. Emotion was pushing me into the Meech camp, reason was pulling me in the other direction. Just as I didn't want Québec to vote itself out of Confederation in May 1980, I didn't want Canada to vote Québec out of Confederation ten years later.

By the time the marathon first ministers' conference started in June 1990, I was a Meech supporter, albeit a reluctant one. I joined the crowd outside the Conference Centre for two evenings and one afternoon, anxiously waiting for the breakthrough that would save Meech and the country. When the breakthrough came, I didn't feel "saved." I felt relieved, as I did the night of the referendum, but not victorious. When the accord died less than two weeks later, I didn't know what to feel.

The debate over Meech Lake should not have surprised us. Or our political leaders. How could Québec be integrated in the constitution when French and English Canadians have fundamentally different versions of the evolution of that constitution?

Version A. French Canadians believe that during the last two hundred years, they have earned a number of constitutional rights: the Quebec Act of 1774 recognized their religion (Roman Catholicism), the seigneurial system of land division and administration, and the French civil code; the Constitutional Act of 1791 gave them a specific territory, Lower Canada, over which they could exercise their growing mastery of the British parliamentary system; the British North America Act of 1867 (now renamed the Constitution Act, 1867) enshrined French and English in the national parliament and in the provincial parliament of Québec; the Constitution Act, 1982, including the Canadian Charter of Rights and Freedoms, further entrenched French-language rights in Canada (although Québec didn't sign that document).

The Meech Lake Accord was designed to secure Québec's signature of the 1982 Constitution Act and is based on five conditions (or "demands," as every opponent of Meech calls them) set by Québec: recognition as a distinct society, a provincial role in appointments to the Supreme Court, a greater provincial role in immigration, limits on federal-provincial shared-cost programs, and a veto for Québec on constitutional amendments.

Version B. Same as Version A except that some English Canadians view these constitutional rights as concessions (undeserved, of course) to French Canadians, with the Meech Lake Accord as the ultimate and unacceptable concession.

The Meech Lake Accord was an attempt to reconcile these two views of Canada, giving Québec a distinct society clause (the constitutional affirmation of the two founding nations) but maintaining "equality" for the other provinces by giving them additional powers.

It would have been kinder to reject Québec's five conditions than to unleash a crisis which has diminished us all.

If the Meech Lake crisis were turned into a board game, it would be called *Blame*. The game would accommodate an infinite number of players, for or against Meech, and could be played indefinitely (no artificial deadline). Québec would be the player to beat, with the largest share of the blame (what else is new?). Blame for:

- its refusal to assimilate during the last two hundred years;
- its rejection of any of the constitutional solutions put forward between 1947 and 1981;
- its refusal to sign the constitution in 1982;
- its five conditions for signing the constitution in 1987;
- its readiness to sign and pass the Meech Lake Accord, which met these five conditions;
- its unwillingness to compromise on the essence of the accord or the deadline;
- its warnings that Québec might leave Confederation if the accord was not ratified.

With a throw of the dice, the blame can be shifted to politicians from every province and every party, depending on your support or opposition to Meech. Blame for:

- masterminding or bungling this whole exercise (Mulroney);
- signing the accord in the first place (Mulroney, Bourassa, Buchanan, Devine, Getty, Ghiz, Hatfield, Pawley, Peckford, Peterson, Vander Zalm);
- passing the legislation in the House of Commons and the Senate (all members who voted for it, including the three party leaders);
- introducing the accord in their provincial legislatures (Bourassa, Buchanan, Devine, Getty, Ghiz, Peckford, Peterson, Vander Zalm);

- passing the accord in these legislatures (all members who voted for it);
- not introducing the accord in their provincial legislatures (Filmon, McKenna);
- aiding and abetting the non-introduction of the accord (Carstairs and Doer of Manitoba);
- rescinding the accord (Wells);
- not compromising on the accord (Bourassa);
- aiding and abetting Bourassa's unwillingness to compromise (Rémillard, Ryan, Parizeau, and the majority of the Québec National Assembly);
- waffling on the accord (the New Democratic Party at its leadership convention, McLaughlin in the House of Commons);
- supporting or rejecting the accord during the leadership campaign for the federal Liberal party (Chrétien, Martin, Copps, Nunziata, Wappel);
- adding fuel to the fire by declaring their cities or towns unilingual English (municipal council members in Sault Ste. Marie, Thunder Bay, and fifty other Ontario municipalities);
- resigning from the federal Conservative caucus over attempts to salvage the accord (Bouchard, Gérin, Chartrand, Nowlan);
- signing Meech II (the eleven first ministers);
- holding up the tabling of the accord in the Manitoba legislature on behalf of the first nations (Elijah Harper);
- finally passing the accord in New Brunswick (McKenna and his fifty-eight member legislature);
- running out of time to pass the accord in the Manitoba Legislative Assembly;
- cancelling the vote on the accord in the Newfoundland House of Assembly (Wells).

Even ex-politicians can be dealt into the game, earning themselves a share of the blame:

- Pierre Elliott Trudeau, for attacking the accord from the time it was signed in 1987;
- Marc Lalonde, Jean Chrétien, Don Johnston and other ex-cabinet ministers for following Trudeau's lead;
- Ed Broadbent, Robert Stanfield, and other ex-politicians for supporting the accord.

The game can accommodate an infinite number of players:

- academics (political scientists and historians in particular);
- the Alliance for the Preservation of English in Canada;
- the Friends of Meech Lake;
- the media (for their zeal in reporting the more negative aspects of the debate);
- pollsters (for endlessly polling the confusion of the public);
- ourselves.

Ourselves. For letting this degenerate into a crisis. For stubbornly refusing to understand one another over the years. For hanging on to our history of grievances against each other. For calling each other names. For allowing politicians to make these crucial decisions without us.

Just when I thought it was safe to be bicultural again. Just when the environment, world peace, and Third World debt seemed to be seeping into our conscience and consciousness. Just when the political map of Europe (east and west) is being redrawn. We resume our silly squabbles.

"Silly squabbles!" both sides cry in outrage. "How dare you call these silly squabbles when the survival of your people is at stake, when the constitution of your country may be forever compromised, when Québec just keeps going too far?" you all yell at me in turn.

I'm sorry but I'm tired of seeing so much political energy wasted on debates over language and who was here first.

I'm tired of hearing fringe groups claim dire consequences for a country that is trying to respect another culture, another language.

I'm tired of having Québec's English language minority

act as if it has a monopoly on moral outrage when it comes to minority-rights violations.

I'm tired of watching our French-language minorities struggle through the courts for recognition of rights they supposedly already have.

I'm tired of our chronic inability to live together.

I'm tired of being tired.

I'm all meeched out.

7. The Legacy of Babel

I am sitting in a Paris restaurant, enjoying a glass of wine before dinner, when two couples arrive and sit at the table next to mine. From their appearance and the bad cut of their clothes, I peg them as East Europeans.

Since the tables are rather close together, I can watch them out of the corner of my eye while seeming to be staring out the window. The woman who is nearest to me is running her fingers over the linen tablecloth, unfolding her napkin, almost with reverence. Sensing that someone is watching her, she looks up. Our eyes meet briefly and we both look away, embarrassed.

The haughty waiter arrives with my veal. I start to eat, trying to keep my eyes off the next table. I soon realize that the people I was watching are now watching me. The four of them are peering over their menus. But I am not the object of their scrutiny, my veal is.

One of them points at my plate and then the menu, wanting to know what I'm eating. I try to tell them in French and then in English but they shake their heads regretfully. When I try German, there is an enthusiastic response from one of the men but his German turns out to be even more basic than mine and his accent difficult to understand.

I tell him that I had the veal (*Kalbfleisch*), and when he tells the others, they all close their menus, relieved that the problem has been solved.

"But there are many marvellous dishes on the menu. Why don't I go through them with you?" I offer, sending the waiter away with a flick of the hand. If my French-Canadian accent offended him, my ability to speak German, even badly, must disgust him.

The woman who was caressing the tablecloth earlier hesitates. She smiles shyly and mutters something to her husband but he shrugs, not knowing the German word.

I try to think of what she might want. Chicken, I ask. He shrugs again. I make some clucking sounds. She smiles.

So we go through the whole menu, mimicking the words we don't know. Like rabbit. Like mushrooms. I try to draw pictures, but my shrimps look like croissants and my asparagus like a Christmas tree with a narrow trunk. My drawings are so bad we all laugh.

The haughty waiter is not impressed. I convey four separate orders, not pointing at the menu, which is what he would have liked me to do, so he could include me in his disdain.

All through the evening, we continue our slow, laborious conversation. I find out that they are Polish, that their names are Anna, Stanislaw, Eva, and Josef, and that the men are bureaucrats, although they won't tell me what they're doing in France.

I show them a picture of my son and they show me pictures of their children. Anna asks me if she can touch my blouse. She works as a seamstress, and she runs her fingers along the sleeve of my blouse as she touched the tablecloth earlier. With reverence. She thinks it's made of silk so I don't tell her it's polyester. Expensive polyester, but a synthetic just the same.

They ask me all kinds of questions, many of which I don't understand, some that I understand but don't know how to explain in German. I am asked about sock pants (pantyhose) and whether my son wore garbage nappies (disposable diapers) when he was a baby.

We all have a brandy together and "talk" for two more hours. When it comes time to part, we are all rather emotional. We know that our paths will never cross again, that, except for our smattering of German, they never would have crossed in the first place. I don't know how they felt about our encounter, but I know I was honoured. To have had a glimpse into their world, to have shared some laughter, to have shared at all.

* * *

LANGUAGE, MORE THAN ANYTHING, CAN TEACH US about people – about diversity, differences. Yet at the same time, give us a way to bridge that diversity, those differences. Full fluency is not required. The German vocabulary I shared with Stanislaw was very basic, the grammar rudimentary, but it enabled five of us to communicate, to eat together, to exchange bits and pieces of our lives.

Languages fascinate me, perhaps because of the price I've had to pay to speak two of them fluently. I've dabbled in three other languages (German, Spanish, and Italian) but they never had the impact on my life that English did.

Learning another language can be a very disruptive, frightening experience, particularly if a child is suddenly thrust into a school environment totally different from what she is accustomed to. This is what often happens to our immigrant children when they are confronted with English or French for the first time. This is what used to happen to Native children when they were sent away to school and punished for speaking their own language.

This was not my experience. My transition to school was very smooth, in terms of both language and community. I didn't suddenly have to understand another language or take a bus to a strange community. I was out of the family nest but still in a familiar tree.

I cannot pinpoint when I first became aware of English as a separate language. Or how I learned it. I lived in a French world surrounded by an English one. I picked English up by osmosis, I guess, on the street, in the classroom, and eventually from books. Although learning English was not a traumatic experience, using it was a great source of ambivalence.

English was a sort of secret language that we rarely admitted to knowing. It wasn't that we were told not to speak it (we just didn't) but that such a fuss was always being made about the quality of our French. Our teachers corrected us for using words common at home (like *catin* for doll, *lunettes* for eyeglasses) and encouraged us to replace them with "better" ones like *poupée* and *verres*. *Joual* was not tolerated nor was *franglais*.

Because I was an excellent student, I was recruited to fight in the front lines, to prove that the French language was not only surviving in Ontario but prospering. It started with that little trophy in grade two, my first bribe. It continued through the years with spelling and grammar drills, essay-writing contests, recitations, and oral improvisations, for which I received gold stars, mimeographed certificates, or holy images. My teachers spent a lot of time grooming me for *le Concours de français*, telling me in grade four that I'd probably be representing the school in grade eight. Telling my closest rivals the same thing so we would all work harder.

Although I was encouraged to excel in French, my insatiable desire to read had long ago exhausted the French books available at our local library. So I turned to English books, fiction as well as history, biography, and geography. At first, I didn't understand half of what I was reading, but the more I read the more I understood. I was both ashamed and proud of my growing vocabulary, a vocabulary I didn't share with anyone. No one even knew I was reading so many English books, since I always hid them under my bed. When I would kneel for prayers in the evening, I would sometimes brush against my hidden treasure and, feeling guilty, ask God for forgiveness.

As my ambivalence about English increased, the pleasure of mastering another language became mixed with feelings of guilt and shame. So, to assuage my guilt, I turned to Latin, a language I could not speak or understand, although I had often memorized it. I tried to decipher Latin texts from my missal, staring at the words for hours as if their meaning or the grammar that joined them together would communicate itself to me. But I soon tired of these exercises in futility and returned to reading all the books I could get my hands on.

When I reached high school, I submerged my guilt feelings

and replaced them with linguistic pretensions. I felt sorry for anyone who didn't know at least two languages. I took Latin (one of the least popular electives) and proceeded to teach myself Spanish from a book. I didn't learn much Spanish, but it was a welcome relief from the French-English tug-of-war inside me.

I didn't realize that the tug-of-war would be a permanent feature of my life. That because of the politics of language in this country my ambivalence about English would continue.

I was also totally unprepared for the consequences of bilingualism, for what happened to my French when I started to speak English on a regular basis.

When you learn another language as a hobby, it has very little impact on your own. It's easy to keep it separate because you use it only under certain circumstances, in the classroom, in the language lab, or with people who are helping you to practise. But if you live in two languages (sometimes by choice, sometimes not), the second language starts to affect your mother tongue. You borrow words from one language to use in the other, you switch from one to another depending on the subject, sometimes in the course of the same conversation.

Verbal communication is a complex neurological process, as anyone who has had a stroke and recovered can attest. Finding the words and conveying them in the right order is something we take for granted. How the words are retrieved from the hundreds in your brain, linked grammatically and coherently, is a mystery to most of us.

I was surprised by the side-effects of bilingualism. Mortified, even. Experts in linguistics have been studying these side-effects for years and have fancy names for them: *interference* (when a word or sentence construction from one language is selected and mixed into another); *lexical borrowing* (when words from one language are imported into another); *language of choice* (the language in which we prefer to discuss a certain subject or address another person); and *code switching* (using two languages at once, often in the same sentence).

I wasn't always aware of this. For years I felt guilty for mixing up my two languages, thinking it was a failure on my part (laziness, not enough vigilance) when it was the way my brain worked. I also felt guilty because I was sometimes more comfortable in my second language than my first. I used to think it was a matter of vocabulary, but now I know it's more complicated than that; it involves complex psychological factors such as the level of comfort, emotional security, and degree of self-esteem associated with each language.

In terms of interference, for example, when a word or phrase from one language gets mixed up with the other, I react differently depending on which language I'm speaking. If I'm speaking in English and a French word or phrase comes to mind, I use it anyway, knowing it will usually trigger the expression I'm looking for. But if I'm speaking in French and an English word comes to mind, I usually freeze in mid-sentence. Why the double standard? Linguistically, exactly the same process has occurred. But because French is my mother tongue, I am ashamed and frustrated when I can't think of the right word right away.

Unilingual people often search for the right word while they're speaking, but because they have only one language, the word that will finally surface is unlikely to be in another.

When I finally realized that the extensive use of two languages affects the way one speaks both languages, I tried to be less hard on myself. I began to accept my bilingualism for the insights it provided instead of dwelling on the technical and emotional difficulties it created in my life.

I didn't choose to learn English, I had to. When I was growing up, we had a saying: the English learn French because they want to; the French learn English because they have to. But now the stakes are much higher.

Outside our borders, English is achieving the status of a universal language. It's becoming the preferred second language in Japan, China, and the Soviet Union. In Europe, South and Central America, and non-anglophone Africa. Even in officially bilingual or multilingual countries like Belgium and Switzerland, many adults are choosing to learn English in addition to the other national languages they learned in school.

The roots of English's growing universality lie in Britain's old colonial empire and America's current domination of world trade. Just as French was the language of diplomacy and German the language of science, English gained currency as the language of trade, acquiring a flexibility and adaptability over the centuries that knows no rival today.

As a long-time user of French and English, I can understand the growing popularity of English. It is flexible and adaptable, even though it has a quirky grammar (what's left of it) and idiosyncratic spelling. Compared to languages with more complex grammars and syntaxes, English has a certain simplicity. It's easy to learn and easy to use, relatively speaking. No accents, no complex declensions, no onerous conjugations.

French, on the other hand, is a complex, precise, and very disciplined language, its integrity zealously protected by l'Académie Française. Because it is more complex, it cannot adapt as easily to rapid change.

This does not make English a "better" language. All languages have their own beauty, their own reason for being. But English has definitely become a useful and practical world language.

A common world language – the fervent dream of the creators of Esperanto – now seems inevitable. That it will be English and not Esperanto is highly probable.

It won't mean the disappearance of other languages, only that more people in the world will speak two of them, their own and English. English-speakers, however, will probably continue to speak only English, lagging behind, as they already do, in second-language learning.

In an EEC study released in 1988, Britain rated last in the community in rates of second-language learning. The United States also has a low rate of second-language learning. Anglophone Americans rarely bother with another language. The majority of Americans who are bilingual have a mother tongue other than English.

Just as Greek and Latin used to be part of a classical education, a second language is mandatory in many countries around the world. In the Third World, it tends to be English, French, or Spanish (depending on that country's colonial past), and the acquisition of that particular language is often an economic necessity. In Europe, it used to be French or German, depending on the political climate at the time, and in Eastern Europe, it was Russian after 1940. As the East Asian countries grow in economic power, the push is to learn English, to trade and compete with America.

It is unfortunate that second-language learning is not the norm in North America, as it is in many countries in Europe. Learning another language is one of life's most educational experiences.

When I was attending an international meeting in Denmark, I was amazed at the number of people in Copenhagen who spoke English – not just the taxi drivers and the shopkeepers, but people I met at bus stops, in elevators, or on street corners. On the plane coming back, I read in an EEC report that Denmark was thinking of making English compulsory from the first grade, with the objective of making all young Danes bilingual by the beginning of the next century.

In Canada, such an objective would be unthinkable. People in non-English-speaking countries can learn English without feeling that they are betraying their own language or culture. In Canada, a French Canadian learning English often feels as if he's giving in, as if she's admitting defeat. I don't know if that can ever be reversed.

English speakers in Canada, the United States, Britain,

Australia, and New Zealand suffer no economic disadvantage by not insisting on second-language education. In fact, the growing universality of English acts as a disincentive for them to bother with other languages. This is unfortunate, for what they don't lose economically, they certainly lose out in perspective. The beauty of language is that it teaches you a new way to see and feel, to think and understand.

I have experienced that at first hand. My proficiency in two languages has considerably expanded my horizons, albeit at an emotional price, a price that merely reflects the politics of language in this country, not the consequences of second-language learning. Every time I learn another language, even if only the basic vocabulary and grammar, I find it opens doors for me, ways of thinking and seeing the world differently.

Learning another language is a humbling experience. It turns an articulate person into a baby with a dictionary. And acquiring vocabulary is only the first step in learning to walk in another language. Knowing all the words won't help you if you can't put them into a sentence that will convey your meaning. You need grammar to form plurals, conjugate verbs, construct relative clauses.

But the vocabulary is the first stumbling block. And you stumble for a long time after you've learned it. I once told a fellow traveller I was taking a skating rink to Switzerland. I meant to say *Eisenbahn* (railway) not *Eisbahn* (skating rink). I should in fact have said *Zug* (train), but that's another story.

Even when you have the dictionary right in front of you, you can select the wrong word. When my mother-in-law, who can speak only German, asked me why I left her son, I tried to tell her I had my reasons. I ended up saying I had grounds, which has a more accusatory connotation, one I didn't intend to make. I had to rely on my ex to explain the misunderstanding that resulted. So much for dictionaries.

The first thing I learned when I was studying Italian was to say, "My name is Lyse. My telephone number is...." One day I finally mustered the courage to use my Italian in a restaurant. The waiter played along and took my order in Italian. When he asked me what my name was, I was so nervous I gave him my name and my phone number as well. The whole sentence came out, word for word. The waiter was flattered (I hope) and I was embarrassed.

Vocabulary errors or grammatical mistakes are nothing compared to a cultural gaffe. I once told a friend of mine from France that she was beautiful as a doll, but I used the word *catin* (which was the word we used for doll when I was growing up) instead of *poupée*. I found out later that in France *catin* means whore.

I became interested in languages because of the price I paid for learning English. Learning other languages relieved the pressure I felt about the two that were tearing my life apart. There was something so liberating about learning Italian just for the sake of learning Italian. When people asked me why I was taking Italian, I told them that it was because I loved opera and pasta. When they pointed out that it wasn't all that useful, that it was only spoken in one country, I just laughed. It was so wonderful to dabble in a new language and not feel guilty about it.

The growing universality of English does not diminish in any way the value of learning other languages. Language is at the very root of our humanity, our need to communicate, to be understood. The legacy of Babel is very real. The existence of hundreds of languages and dialects has obscured the basic universality of language, that basic human need to communicate. If we can achieve a world language that can permit more direct communication between people, all well and good. But to undo the legacy of Babel, we have to teach respect and tolerance for all languages. And there is no better way to instil that tolerance and respect than through the teaching of other languages.

8. The Politics of Language

A t a small airport outside London, England, I encounter a young Canadian couple from Victoria, B.C. It is the day after the May 1979 election, and Joe Clark is now the prime minister of Canada. Noticing the Air Canada tag on my luggage, they are eager to discuss the election results with me.

"The first thing the Conservatives have to do is dismantle official bilingualism," the young man says. His wife nods vigorously, her lips barely concealing a sneer.

I don't tell them I'm French Canadian, and I don't challenge their opinion.

The reason we even meet is that the small chartered plane we were supposed to take to Paris is having engine trouble and we've been stranded in Lytton's inadequate airport lounge for hours.

It is evening by the time Dan-Air, which we've now nicknamed Ban-Air, finally informs us that they cannot repair the plane and will be bussing and ferrying us to Paris. On the bus to Dover, the young couple sit in front of me, eager to resume our discussion – or should I say their discussion.

"Joe Clark has a tough job ahead of him. It will take him years to undo all the damage Trudeau has inflicted on the rest of the country."

"Official bilingualism is officially dead. No more shoving French down Western throats."

I listen with more sadness than anger. Here on a quiet English country road, I have to listen to the same old diatribes. Next time, I'll make sure to snip the Air Canada tags off my luggage.

The irony is that I have been to British Columbia and they've never been east of Calgary (except to fly over Canada to England). I know a lot of British Columbian history, probably more than they do.

In Dover, we board the last hovercraft to France. In Calais, the bus that is to take us to Paris is nowhere to be found.

"Typical French. No consideration for people," the woman from Victoria mutters under her breath, but loud enough for me to hear. I remind her that Dan-Air, which is British, got us into this mess in the first place. She glares at me and pops her gum.

The bus has been delayed and we have to wait for almost two hours, huddled in the hallway of the ferry terminal building, which is now closed. We reach Paris at 5:30 in the morning, dumped unceremoniously in front of the Dan-Air office in a Paris suburb. There is no one from the airline to meet us; the office is dark and empty. We paid £35 to fly from London to Paris in an hour, and it has taken us almost twenty hours to get here. And the young man from Victoria thinks our airline system should be deregulated.

Since I'm the only one in the group who speaks French, I'm expected to rescue everyone. Most people had hotel reservations for the night before and are at a loss as to what to do – especially the couple from Victoria. (Their whole trip was arranged by a travel agent, hotel, train reservations, everything.)

And who helps them? Who telephones the hotels and finds them rooms at that ungodly hour, who finds the subway station and shows them how to get tickets when all the instructions are in French? Who helps them find a currency exchange?

I do. So much for shoving French down their throats.

* * *

NO ONE KNOWS EXACTLY HOW MANY LANGUAGES there are in the world. Current estimates range from 3,000 to 6,000, with much debate as to what is classified as language or dialect.

Ranking can be done in many ways. In terms of languages spoken by the most people, the top six are, in order: Chinese, English, Hindi-Urdu, Russian, Spanish, and Arabic (French is tenth). In terms of official or national status, there are four languages that dominate, by number of countries, not number of speakers: English is an official or national language in forty-seven countries, French in twenty-six, Arabic in twenty-one, and Spanish in nineteen.

In Canada, we think we have problems because we recognize two languages, both of which are spoken by millions of people around the world. In Papua, New Guinea (pop. 3,900,000), they acknowledge English, Melanesian pidgin, Hiri Motu, and 717 distinct native languages.

Canada is not the only country with linguistic and cultural tensions. In the United Kingdom, languages other than English have almost disappeared (some would say they were systematically eradicated), but the cultural differences remain almost three hundred years after unification (1701). In France, there are linguistic and cultural tensions, not only in the Breton and Basque regions, but also in Alsace and Corsica. The United States has a growing Hispanic minority (almost 20 per cent of California's population of 26 million, 55 per cent of the city of Miami's) that is becoming more vocal in its demands.

Other countries have more than one official language. Although India has two official languages, Hindi and English, twelve others (among them Bengali, Urdu, and Punjabi) are recognized in its constitution. Switzerland has three official languages (German, French, Italian) and one recognized language (Romansch). Yugoslavia has three official languages (Serbo-Croatian, Slovene, Macedonian), Belgium two (French and Flemish), and Finland two (Finnish and Swedish).

In the Soviet Union as a whole, Russian is the official language, but each of the fifteen republics has its own official language in which it conducts its affairs. There are also more than one hundred regional languages.

In some other countries, there are combinations of official and national languages, two or more languages that are recognized but with different status.

"Official" bilingualism or multilingualism does not make the inhabitants of these countries bilingual or multilingual. It is often just an official recognition of existing linguistic minorities within the country. Countries that are officially unilingual – like the United States, for example – can have many bilingual people, sometimes more than an officially bilingual country.

In spite of more than twenty years of official bilingualism and French immersion, when French and English Canadians meet, it is almost always French Canadians who end up speaking English. French Canadians make up the majority of people in Canada who are bilingual in French and English.

There are of course many other bilingual people in Canada. People who speak their mother tongue as well as one of Canada's official languages, sometimes even both of them. That mother tongue may be a European, African, or Asian language, or an aboriginal language native to Canada. In our obsession with official bilingualism, we often deny that reality. Saying that only such and such a percentage of people are bilingual when we mean bilingual in French and English. I know of one public servant who is constantly referred to as unilingual because he has no French when he in fact speaks four languages (English, Czech, German, and Russian).

In most countries with official languages, speakers of those languages are usually located within a given territory. In Belgium, Flemings occupy the north and west of the country, the French the south and east. Brussels, however, is mostly French although it is located in Flemish territory. In Switzerland, most cantons are unilingual, very few are bilingual. Only federal services are trilingual; cantonal services are usually unilingual.

In Canada, only Québec has a French majority, and for many years its economy was dominated by the English minority. Two adjoining provinces, Ontario and New Brunswick, are home to 76 per cent of the remaining French-speaking Canadians. The other 24 per cent are scattered throughout Canada.

Language doesn't divide us, the politics of language do. The language itself is rarely the issue. Equality of treatment, a share of the political power, these are the real issues behind minority demands. The same applies to the recognition of religious, ethnic, or regional differences.

Language is a powerful symbol, and in Canada the use of French is the yardstick by which a whole culture measures its survival. It has also become the symbol of Québec's political clout and therefore attracts all the resentment such clout generates.

Québec's political clout is based on population (first and foremost) and on homogeneity, not language. United in their struggle for cultural survival, the people of Québec have tended to vote *en bloc* more often than those of other provinces. It has therefore always been essential for any federal party to win a substantial number of seats in Québec in order to win a majority. But it is Québec's population, second only to Ontario's, that gives it the clout it has. Not the fact that it's French.

Linguistic duality is our sacred cow, our Achilles' heel, our albatross. It distorts our history, our politics, our views of ourselves. Which is ironic considering how much of an illusion it really is.

In spite of official bilingualism, there are only two provinces that have linguistic duality, Québec (although it is now "officially" unilingual French) and New Brunswick. The lives of French minorities in the rest of Canada have not been substantially altered by official bilingualism at the federal level. Being able to buy a stamp in French or to fill out a French income-tax form has very little impact on the day-to-day lives of French minorities. These are more affected by provincial and municipal jurisdictions, which aren't bilingual (health, education, courts, recreation, arts and culture).

In New Brunswick, Canada's only officially bilingual province, the situation has improved over the last twenty years, although those improvements have now prompted the formation of the Confederation of Regions Party, which wants to halt that progress, even reverse it. Ontario's Bill 8, for all its good intentions, is only beginning to address the needs of a minority that has seen its numbers drop from 15 per cent of the province's population in 1960 to 5 per cent in 1989. It's a blood transfusion that might come too late to save the patient.

The situation in the rest of the country does not offer much hope. In 1988, Saskatchewan and Alberta more or less declared themselves unilingual (Bill 2 and Bill 60 respectively). An Alberta MLA, Léo Piquette, was kicked out for speaking French in the Legislative Assembly. Imagine the uproar if an MNA from Québec was expelled for speaking English!

And when there is a ray of hope, like the Supreme Court decision that found in favour of a French parents' group in Edmonton who wanted to control their own schools, it is not granted by the government but wrestled from it through the courts. That seems the only way the French minorities can win the rights that everyone assumes they already have, by going to court – a long, expensive, and painful process.

Québec's English minority, in the meantime, has its own hospitals, school boards, universities, legal and other professional services, newspapers, television, and radio. And the all-out support of the majority of Canadians in their struggle for their "rights."

The rights of the French majority in Québec receive no such outside support, even when they are enshrined in legislation that has the whole-hearted backing of that majority: La Charte de la langue (Bill 101).

The Québec government now finds itself in a catch-22 situation where that legislation is concerned. The growing universality of English outside Canada means that more and more immigrants who will come to Québec will already have English as a second language and will be even more reluctant to send their children to French schools, as the law requires. On the other hand, Québec's dynamic economy needs more skilled workers, therefore more immigrants. Québec's expanding economy is also bringing the Québécois into closer and closer contact with the world marketplace, which is more English than ever.

Bill 101 requires the children of immigrants to attend French schools, but their growing numbers in the city of Montréal (estimated at 40 per cent of the school population) have created problems unforeseen by the drafters of the law. High school students are confronting each other, the French demanding that French be spoken in the hallways and in the schoolyard and their classmates insisting that they have the right to speak English or their own language.

The Montréal Catholic School Commission is contemplating regulations to force these children to speak French at all times on school property. There's also been talk of limiting the number of non-francophones to 30 per cent per school by bussing children around or creating "separate" schools for them.

These students are not allowed to attend English schools. They do, however, have a life of their own outside school, a life in which they converse in Chinese, Spanish, English, or whatever. When can an individual's freedom of speech (in this case, freedom to speak in the language of one's choice) infringe on the majority's right to survive in another language?

Trying to save the language of the majority can lead to racist and discriminatory practices. Such are the dilemmas of language laws. Instead of condemning Québec's actions in this area, or assuming that Québec will do "the wrong thing," we should try first to understand what is at stake. Because, as the demographics in our urban areas change, we may face similar problems in the future. English-speaking students may one day find themselves in classes where the majority are learning English as a second language.

At my son's school, they are very strict about the rule that students should speak French in the hallways and schoolyard. I'm not crazy about the zeal with which they sometimes apply this policy, but I accept it as the price to pay for preserving my son's French in a predominantly English environment.

Sometimes I wonder why I even bother trying to understand the dilemmas faced by Québec, why I care what happens to Québec. Because in the last ten years, Québec has done little to offer support for French minorities struggling outside its borders.

When Saskatchewan declared itself unilingual, the premier of Québec said little, anxious not to upset the Meech Lake apple cart. I guess Québec feels it has to put itself first (which is what every province does) and can't afford to use any of its precious clout to defend the rights of its poor cousins.

We never expected more than moral support, but that moral support has been sadly lacking. Perhaps Québec thinks that, if it protects its language and culture, all French minorities will ultimately benefit. Unfortunately, every time Québec passes legislation to protect its majority, the other provinces jump to the defence of Québec's English minority, conveniently ignoring the plight of their own French-speaking minority.

When Ontario municipalities started passing resolutions declaring themselves unilingual English, Québec saw these declarations not as anti-French but as anti-Québec. These resolutions, although influenced by the fall-out from Bill 178, were in reaction to Ontario legislation (Bill 8), legislation that had been passed three years earlier and was only then going into effect. Québec, in its haste to mobilize any anti-French feeling and bolster its stand on Meech Lake, ignored the fact that these declarations were aimed at Ontario's French minority, not at Québec (which would in no way be affected).

As a member of that French minority, I was appalled by these unilingual declarations and by the animosity with which they were made. I was ashamed to live in Ontario, to have fooled myself into thinking I was welcome in this province, my province. The city councils that passed these resolutions insisted that they were not anti-French, that they were only motivated by economic considerations – their inability to afford French services. Yet they knew full well that Bill 8 did not require them to provide such services.

Ontario has the largest number of francophones outside the province of Québec, about half a million people, most of whom are concentrated in eastern and northern Ontario. It has been a rather docile minority, concentrating its efforts on improving the quality of education for its children. Half a million people, a mere 5 per cent of the population, a tiny minority indeed. But wait a minute, that's more than three times the population of Prince Edward Island, a little less than the population of Newfoundland, two-thirds the population of New Brunswick, or half the population of provinces like Manitoba and Saskatchewan. Not so insignificant in Canadian terms, after all.

When Bill 178 was passed in Québec, a bill dealing with the language of commercial signs, there was an incredible outcry from the rest of Canada. But when municipalities in Canada's richest, most powerful province, declared themselves unilingual, with bigoted comments freely exchanged during the debate preceding these declarations, there was very little outcry outside Ontario and Québec.

There are now two views of Canada competing for attention: the vision of twenty years ago, of a bilingual, multicultural country; and the vision of competing unilingualisms – French in Québec, English in the rest of Canada, with safeguards for minorities in both.

I don't even know which one I prefer any more, which one I would support if there were a referendum on the matter. Maybe we need a new vision, a totally different way of looking at the country. Canada is, after all, still very young.

We seem to have a mediocrity complex, an innate ability to wallow in our own squabbles. In the months that saw the tumbling of the Berlin Wall, the disembowelling of the Communist Party in the Soviet Union, and the release of Nelson Mandela in South Africa, Ontario municipalities were declaring themselves unilingual English and the youth wing of the Parti Québécois was on a scavenger hunt in Hull, looking for apostrophes on commercial signs.

Maybe it's time to shed that mediocrity complex, to end our silly squabbles once and for all.

9. Double Duty in the Public Service

This has become a daily ritual, Dave and Ron hanging around the water cooler making comments about frogs. I wonder if they were as preoccupied with frogs before I came to work here. Maybe it's just because I'm new. Because I'm their first real live French Canadian. Some kind of initiation rite.

If only the water cooler weren't so close to the files. I try not to listen to what they're saying, but the harder I try, the more acute my hearing seems to become. I swear, sometimes I can hear them breathe. From several feet away.

"I wonder if we should keep this cooler in here now that the froggy invasion has started. I mean, we'll have to be real careful. Wouldn't want to have frog eggs in the water, now, would we? Or frog shit."

Why doesn't Joe say something? He's the supervisor, he could put them in their place. Why doesn't anyone else say anything? They either feel the same or they're cowards. Like me.

I would love to walk over there, take some water and say something witty like "Frog shit would improve the taste." But my legs won't take me, the words just limp around in my mouth.

"I guess these little paper cups will come in handy. In case one of them frogs gets into the cooler for a little swim, you know what I mean? We can scoop him out and crush him right in the cup, like this. That way we won't get slimed or nothing."

* * *

THAT INCIDENT HAPPENED A LONG TIME AGO. Whenever I think about it, I have visions of the little frog exploding in Dave's big hand, its tiny guts all over the place, its little skin, empty and limp, hanging out of the paper cup.

My sister and I used to play with frogs a lot, at my grandparents' cottage. We kept about fifty of them in an old sunken row-boat that was just deep enough to prevent the frogs from jumping out. We spent hours playing with them, talking to them, pretending they were talking to us.

So when Dave crushed the paper cup, I was more concerned about his imaginary frog than his reference to French Canadians. More concerned about my silence, my cowardice, than his bigotry.

I remind myself of that incident sometimes, to confirm that attitudes at the office have changed. Comments about frogs are rare these days, although ethnic jokes about other groups are still popular.

Working as a federal public servant only heightens my cultural schizophrenia, making me travel between the solitudes on a day-to-day basis. Putting me in constant contact with English Canadians who think French is being shoved down their throats and French Canadians who think I've sold out.

Bilingualism in the workplace. Is it possible to describe the difficulties of working in two languages without sounding like the princess who couldn't sleep because there was a pea under her fifteen mattresses?

I would have liked to dispel the notion that bilingual people "have it made" in the public service. That they get all the jobs, that they get all the breaks. But such notions are rarely dispelled, based as they are on opinion rather than numbers, resentment rather than reality.

I have learned over the last twenty years that the implementation of official bilingualism in the workplace is never simple, never easy. That it makes an already difficult job more difficult. That attitudes change slowly, if at all.

Being bilingual in the public service isn't easy. For it's the bilingual public servants, most of them francophones, who bear the burden of the Official Languages Act and the brunt of the resentment. We get to do our job twice, once in English, once in French.

Every step we take up the ladder is attributed to our

bilingualism, not our other qualifications, years of hard work, or personal suitability.

Our ability to speak and write French and understand Québec issues is sometimes exploited by managers who need our skills but reject the persons we are, the persons we had to be, to be this bilingual.

Just as women find it hard to fit into the corporate culture, francophone public servants often find it hard to adjust to the mentality of their anglophone bosses.

I remember once having to draft a highly confidential letter, the object of which was to avert the resignation of an official that might be embarrassing to the government. I was only involved because the letter had to be in French and everyone in the chain of command from the minister's office down to me was anglophone.

My instructions were clear. The letter had to be perfect, both in presentation and in content. It had to be graceful, reassuring, and allow the man to save face (he apparently didn't really want to resign but felt he had no choice). And since the letter might be made public, the promises had to be less than specific. A tall order.

When I handed my boss the letter the next morning, he read it (his French reading skills were passable) and said:

"I knew you could do it. Just the kind of sentimental bullshit a Frenchie will go for. Good job."

I stood in front of his desk for the longest time without saying anything. He shuffled his papers, pretending I wasn't there. I stared at him until he looked at me.

"I worked very hard on that letter. In fact, I'm the only person on your staff who could have written it. Remember that the next time you need help from this 'Frenchie'."

I joined the civil service (as it was still called then) as a clerk in 1969, the same year the Official Languages Act came into effect. I doubt whether I was aware of this legislation, or of the tremendous impact it would one day have on my work life.

The impact it would have on your work life, ha! I can hear disgruntled anglophones muttering in the background. Don't be disgruntled, my friends. I share your sense of frustration. What I want to illustrate is that bilingualism is not easy for anyone.

There is no doubt in my mind that my fluency in both official languages has made me highly employable. The irony is that, although I'm hired because I'm bilingual, I still do much of my work in English. Call it expediency, call it efficiency, there is usually not much choice. When my boss is unilingual, I don't think it makes much sense to write my reports in French and have them translated into English so we can discuss them together.

Only these days, my decision to write a report in English for the sake of expediency is often viewed as a concession, as an abdication of my right to work in the language of my choice. For the politics of language have seeped inevitably into the public service, creating a microcosm of the country's linguistic tensions.

Federal government employees do not live in a vacuum. They live in the same world other Canadians do and don't leave their opinions about language with the commissionaire when they arrive in the morning.

Their opinions spill over in the workplace. As tensions mount on the outside, the language of work becomes symbolic of the larger struggle. I receive disapproving glances when I reply in English instead of French to a question posed to me in English, during the course of a bilingual meeting. One of my bilingual memos is returned because the French text isn't first (i.e., on the left), with my name circled and the word *vendue* written beside it. I have my French corrected during a presentation by a know-it-all who thinks I've used an anglicism. I get little sermons about how I should stand up for my rights and force the English to speak to me in French.

Even at work, I'm supposed to take sides.

As long as the emphasis was on service to the public, I was safe. The client determined my language of work: which language I spoke to him, used to reply to her letter, spoke at their meetings. But one of the other provisions of the Official Languages Act allows public servants to work in the language of their choice. The act is very clear about whose choice it is; the individual public servant's. But for people like me, that is little consolation.

I quite regularly switch from French to English to accommodate my colleagues. I never address my French-speaking colleagues in English or my English-speaking colleagues in French, unless they've asked me to, because they want to practise their other language, or because they're more comfortable in one than the other, or whatever. I respect their wishes.

If I'm in a meeting and someone asks me a question, I answer in the language in which the question was posed. Some of my francophone colleagues disagree with that, feeling that I should answer in French on principle. Let the others struggle.

As a professional communicator, I have a problem with that approach. If someone asks me a question in English, I would rather answer her in English. How I respond, including the language I respond in, is as important as what I say. And if someone asks me a question in French, I would never dream of responding in English.

If I think that several people in the room have not understood my reply, I sometimes paraphrase it in the other language as well. Some people think this is pandering. I think it's just good communications.

I once had a minister who liked to work in French only. Having worked for many ministers who wanted to work in English only, it was a nice change. This minister would regularly write to his provincial and territorial colleagues in French. I think that he was proving a point but not scoring any. The purpose of his letter was to communicate, to consult with his colleagues. By sending it in French only, he was being as insensitive as all the ministers who regularly write to their colleague in Québec in English only.

The most difficult thing about working in a bilingual environment is that true equality of language is not possible. In the day-to-day realities of getting the job done, one language gets sacrificed over the other. For example, a French-speaking employee may lose an argument because she isn't able to express herself as convincingly in English. An English-speaking employee may miss out being assigned to a project because the team is mostly French-speaking and the working document will be in French.

Because English is still the majority language, the language that gets sacrificed most often is French. And nowhere more often than in writing. Which brings us to the subject of translation.

It is perhaps difficult for a unilingual person to understand how complex translation is. It's not just a matter of finding the corresponding words, stringing them into sentences, and returning them to the owner of the original text. Meaning is not only conveyed with words but with grammar and syntax, as well as in more subtle ways, like the use of the active voice rather than the passive, the strength of a verb, the selection of adjectives or adverbs. Every language has its own mechanisms for conveying meaning, emphasis, and degree.

In a working document that is just trying to convey facts about a certain subject, the quality of the translation may not be crucial. But when the document is trying to convince the reader or clarify a crucial issue, the translated text is as important as the original.

Translators have two disadvantages when tackling a text. The most insidious is time, or lack of it. Deadlines for translation are rarely generous. The other disadvantage is that translators are not privy to the knowledge that the writer of the original text had. So when they come across an ambiguous passage, they often have to guess at what the author meant, the tight deadline making it impossible to check back and forth with the writer of the original document. If the passage is particularly dense, the guessing becomes cumulative.

When major documents are planned, the preparation of the original document (usually in English) gets the most generous deadline, let's say two weeks, a month; the translation, a few days. The translated document is not given the same consideration as the original. Not that the translation needs the same amount of time, just more time than is usually allotted.

Unilingual public servants send their documents to translation and wait for them to come back. Bilingual public servants are often expected to produce their work in both languages. Unilinguals cannot check whether the translation faithfully renders their thoughts or arguments. Bilingual public servants check their documents and revise them if necessary. Yet bilingual and unilingual public servants work the same hours, are expected to produce the same output. Where does the double duty fit in?

The Official Languages Act affects my work life every single day. Since I deal in information, the dilemma is always which language to use in developing a document or publication. Depending on who will be providing the information for the document and who will be approving the final text, you choose the most practical language. Knowing that, in the end, the original version of the publication will be better than the translated one.

A translation is a translation is a translation. This is a truism we have to live with. Since much of the work in the federal government is still done in English first, most French government documents are translations.

What's your problem, they're available in French, aren't they? Yes, but availability isn't everything. Always reading a language in translation can be tedious and frustrating.

Every once in a while, I circulate an English translation of a French document before it has been revised. When people start complaining about the poor quality of the English, the short choppy sentences, I tell them not to worry, that they're reading a translation. Remind them that francophones have to read that quality of French all the time.

French and English are not very compatible languages, which makes translation trickier. When you're translating languages that have similar grammar and sentence structures (let's say Spanish and French), the transition to the other language is smoother. But in terms of sentence structure and syntax, English and French don't have a lot in common. So it's not a matter of words. Most words have an equivalent in the other language, but the way the sentence is put together, the length of it, the placement of subordinate clauses, and the use of punctuation complicate the translation, and the transition to the other language is rough and self-conscious.

Shouldn't a good translator be able to fix that? It's not that simple. If he or she has enough time to do a proper revision, the text can be improved. But it's still a translation. It's still not the way it would have been written if it had been done in that language in the first place. It's still a matter of fitting a square peg into a round hole.

The greatest hardship for me is to try to maintain the integrity of my first language. Every time I use English at work, my French suffers because it's not being used. If I make a special effort to work only in French, I end up reading translated French all the time. Which only makes it more difficult for me to keep my French untainted.

Although I still write very well in French, I know the quality of my French has been affected, that some of my sentence structures are English rather than French, that some of my expressions are translations and not idiomatic.

It's one of the ironies of the government's language training program that anglophones are taught French and francophones English, but there is no support for bilingual people, mostly francophone, who are trying to maintain the integrity and quality of their mother tongue.

That particular irony was brought home to me again

recently when I heard someone, in an official capacity, claim that anglophones were being denied an opportunity to practise their hard-earned French skills. He urged francophones to make a special effort to help them work in French. I think francophones already carry most of the burden of the Official Languages Act. They don't have time to worry about their colleagues who are trying to maintain their second-language skills, they are too busy trying to do their jobs in two languages and maintain their own first language.

The federal public service would seem like the ideal work environment for a bicultural Canadian like me, an opportunity to work in both cultures, to use both languages every day. But it's not that simple. Although public servants are supposed to be neutral, we all know that neutrality is not really possible. Every thinking person is political, has opinions. The public servants who work in Ottawa come from every region of Canada and bring with them a variety of attitudes and perceptions about the federal government and its policies. Working for the federal government does not alter their attitudes or perceptions, does not change their opinions. In many cases, it just reinforces them, convincing these public servants that Ottawa really doesn't understand their province.

Working in the public service has sensitized me to regional concerns, opened my eyes to the perceptions outside the Toronto-Ottawa-Montréal triangle. In working with colleagues who grew up in the Prairies or the Maritimes, British Columbia or the North, I have come to appreciate how they view Ottawa, how they perceive Ontario and Québec. Travelling across the country, trying to explain one federal program or another, has generated other insights. It's an ongoing process as the issues change, as economic circumstances change. (I have also attended numerous federal-provincial meetings, listening as the various provinces take up their positions, seeing the Québec representative almost always isolated because his or her agenda is different from everyone else's.)

For one particular program, I travelled once a year to every provincial capital to collect feedback from my provincial counterparts. I would start off in St. John's and make my way west over a period of about fourteen days. I would read the paper in each city and watch the national and local news in my hotel room. Sometimes a news story would break while I was in one capital and I would follow it from province to province. After a while, I wasn't sure I was on the same planet, let alone in the same country.

I now feel I have a good sense of this country, of the various concerns that affect the regions. Of the tremendous challenge that faces the government in dealing with such a variety of economies and problems.

I also have a good sense of how bitter Canadians are over bilingualism. I work with anglophones who feel their careers have been severely curtailed by bilingualism, with francophones who think they are being overworked, with scorekeepers on both sides. I listen to irate Westerners who think bilingualism is too expensive and an infringement of their rights, to impatient Québécois who think our documents are not translated fast enough, or well enough, or that they don't reflect their views.

No, working in the public service is not the ideal environment for a bicultural, not a bicultural like me, at any rate. It's just one more place to get caught in the middle.

10. Solitudes, Mosaics, and Melting Pots

I am chewing on a piece of smoked whale meat, regretting I ever put my hand in the bowl on the coffee table. Not that I tried the salty, blubbery morsel out of obligation or politeness; I genuinely like to try different foods. But I've been chewing on this piece for ten minutes, and I'm afraid I'll choke if I swallow it whole.

I finally spit it out into a napkin and take another piece, much smaller this time, unwilling to admit defeat. Susie is sipping on her third beer and playing footsie with the host.

"Why are you eating that shit?" she mutters under her breath. "Dan probably puts it out so whities like you can lap it up as a cultural experience."

Dan is Susie's Inuit friend. Susie is originally from Toronto, but she's lived much of her adult life in the North.

"Why did you bring me here? Just to make fun of me and call me a whitie? I feel conspicuous enough already."

"It's a party, Lyse, not a tribal ceremony. Act like you would at any party. Have a beer. Listen to the music. Stop behaving like a damn anthropologist."

Susie was an anthropology major until she dropped out of university. Calling someone an "anthropologist" is her most scathing put-down. It's her way of telling me I'm a fake, of implying I live a vicarious life.

The room is filled with smoke, not all of it tobacco smoke, and loud music. The younger Inuit guests, who are attending school in Ottawa, are into heavy metal and one of them has plugged his electric guitar into the stereo's amplifier.

The music stops abruptly when a man and a woman, in traditional costume, are ushered into the room. They are both very stooped and seem uncomfortable with all the attention their entrance has generated. Someone introduces them and explains that they are in Ottawa for a special ceremonial dance.

Since Susie seems to have disappeared, I ask the man next to me if he knows anything about these people or the special

ceremonial dance. He shrugs. "Just a bunch of old seals per-
forming for southerners," he says contemptuously.

When the music starts up again, the old couple seem
bothered by the noise. I watch them out of the corner of my
eye, wishing I had the nerve to go and talk to them. That would
be presumptuous of me, I guess. They are not walking artefacts
that I can just pump for information, like a computer module in
a museum.

Supper is served. Caribou stew and arctic char. I try
everything, proud of my "broad" taste. But I feel alone, isolated.

Susie hasn't resurfaced. "Last I heard she was necking
with Dan," someone informs me.

I leave the party shortly after, bewildered, and ashamed of
my failure to make any real contact.

❈ ❈ ❈

SUSIE WAS PARTLY RIGHT. I WAS A "WHITIE," BUT
not by choice. I was naive and anxious to socialize and maybe
that was offensive. But as a human being, what else could I
do but start with rituals that I knew: sharing food, making
conversation?

It took me a while to realize that Susie had wanted me to
be a "whitie," so that she could continue to be the one that was
different. The white woman that talked tough, that could
ridicule whites with the best of them. She herself was an
"anthropologist."

How many of us have ever had real contact with people of
the First Nations? Apart from Native people selling moccasins
and beadwork at craft shows or Inuit artists giving soapstone-
carving demonstrations? Much of what we know about their
way of life is gleaned from museum artefacts, Native art, and
the analyses of ethnologists and curators. Much of what we
know about their problems is gleaned from news items or

television documentaries, hardly the most reliable sources of information on other human beings.

We don't even know what to call them any more. There are so many labels out there, Amerindians, aboriginal peoples, Native people, Indians, Inuit, Dene. But whatever we call them, we have an abundance of perceptions about the way they live, some positive (harmony with nature, artistic expression, extended families), but mostly negative (alcohol and drug abuse, violence, high suicide and infant-mortality rates).

We claim to appreciate their art, yet we display their works at the Canadian Museum of Civilization as artefacts instead of at the National Gallery as works of art. We have romantic notions about their traditional way of life and bleeding-heart-liberal *Angst* about the poverty on their reserves.

There are many solitudes in Canada, although we seem obsessed by only two of them, the French and the English.

The two solitudes. The most enduring cliché of the Canadian condition, with cultural mosaic coming a close second. English-Canadian clichés, that is. Our metaphors, like our languages, are not interchangeable.

Do the First Nations have metaphors about their isolation? Do metaphors as we know them even exist in their languages? Do Canadians from other ethnic backgrounds appreciate having their experiences and those of their ancestors grouped together under that other metaphor-turned-cliché, the cultural mosaic?

What do those clichés say about our country and how we came together, about our society and how we integrate newcomers?

I don't know how we talked about Canada before Hugh MacLennan wrote his novel *Two Solitudes*, in which he chronicled the differences in the lives of his French- and English-Canadian characters. His title was inspired by a passage from a German poet, Rainer Maria Rilke: "Love consists in this, that two solitudes protect, and touch, and greet each other."

Although the book was published in 1945, I don't know exactly when the term *two solitudes* became the cliché for the relationship between Canada's French and English communities. It certainly displaced Lord Durham's famous comment, that Upper and Lower Canada were "two nations warring in the bosom of a single state" (1839).

The mosaic approach was proposed as early as 1922 and became a catchword for cultural pluralism in the thirties. *Plural mosaic, cultural mosaic, Canadian mosaic*, there have been many variations over the years. When John Porter wrote his classic work on Canada's ethnic pecking order in 1965, he dubbed it *The Vertical Mosaic*.

In *Two Solitudes*, MacLennan was distinctly referring to English Canadians of British descent. The "English" solitude of today seems to include nine million Canadians who are not of British ancestry. A formidable solitude indeed.

Each solitude claims to be misunderstood by the other. Québec, however, claims to misunderstand less, to understand English Canada better than English Canada understands Québec. It is true that most English Canadians don't seem to understand Québec. But the mistake that Québec makes is to think there is an English Canada to understand. Because there isn't. The English Canada they claim to understand is represented by the English Quebecker who lives in Westmount or his counterpart in Toronto. There are other types of English-speaking Quebeckers, other types of Torontonians. And what does Québec know of Newfoundlanders or British Columbians of British descent? And if the second solitude encompasses all non-French Canadians, what does Québec know about Saskatchewan's ethnic mix or Manitoba's?

The two-solitudes notion persists because we are so obsessed with linguistic duality, because dividing people up by language has become second nature to us. That is why I object to the use of terms like francophone, anglophone and allophone (used mostly in Québec to denote non-French and non-English speakers). What am I? A franglophone? This kind of categorization is a form of class system based on language rather than economic circumstances, and just as unfair. It's worse than hyphenation (as in Italian-Canadian or Chinese-Canadian), grouping people by language rather than culture and, in the case of allophones, grouping all "others" under one label.

What we should remember about the two solitudes is the word *solitude*. As in loneliness, isolation, separateness. Does that sound like a society to you, where two lonely people live side by side, misunderstanding each other, not knowing that down the street there are other lonely people, people they've forgotten in their obsession with one another?

We have rejected the melting pot and replaced it with other images of a diverse society. The cultural mosaic, each tile a tiny but essential fragment of the larger picture. A rich tapestry, where strands from every ethnic group are woven into the Canadian national fabric to make it strong.

The melting pot can't compete with those kinds of images. The melting pot is a pejorative analogy: boiling everything down to a thin broth, stripping all ingredients of their texture, flavour.

A mosaic is made up of many different tiles, in different sizes and colours. When you look at it closely, you can see only the individual tiles; when you stand back, you can see the pattern, the larger picture. I guess if you stand back far enough from the Canadian mosaic, you're supposed to see a maple leaf. I see a large question mark.

What worries me about the mosaic analogy is that, although the tiles make up the whole, they are cemented to the wall in isolation, their sides not touching. You can almost see them struggling to pry themselves loose and get close to one another. In the melting pot getting close is not a problem. I am not advocating a melting pot philosophy (heresy of heresies), only a little less smugness about the cultural mosaic.

But cultural clichés are not only general, they are also personal and specific, as in the all-too-common ethnic stereotype. I fight that kind of stereotype all the time. People think that because I'm French Canadian, I come from Québec, I'm Catholic, I vote Liberal (although after the last federal election, they'll peg me a Conservative), I like *poutine* and maple syrup, drink Pepsi and beer, watch hockey on television, and go to Florida in the winter and Maine in the summer. Except for the maple syrup and the religion (although I'm not a practising Catholic), wrong on all counts.

I am not an expert on cultural diversity, only an interested bystander. I have always been fascinated by other cultures, fancying myself as a kind of cultural observer, a voyeur more likely (or is it *voyeuse*?). I don't know where this curiosity comes from. Perhaps it's a by-product of being bicultural.

But of course you can't really observe culture, not even your own. Because it's not something you can see or feel, it's a complex layering of different influences, unique to each individual. And people don't project all their layers at once, not even to themselves.

In trying to find an anecdote to illustrate this chapter, I came across many fragments, but nothing definitive, just moments in my life where I was given a glimpse of another culture, another way of life, including strangely enough, a glimpse back into my own.

I was only ever in a synagogue once, for a bar mitzvah. As an avid student of literature and history, I had read much about the Jews, their religion, their culture, the tragedy of the Holocaust. But this was different, this was real, this ceremony was for my neighbours' son. Although I was not unfamiliar with the significance of the ceremony, the language and the gestures were foreign to me. I watched with great interest, wishing I knew what that particular passage meant, or that exchange, or that gesture. As I witnessed this solemn occasion, I was reminded that my life had once centred on other sacred rituals. Sunday Mass, Holy Communion, novenas, *Te Deums*, and stations of the cross.

In a sterile office, half a city away, I had to deal with sacred rituals of another ancient people. Only I hadn't read their literature, knew nothing about their history, and knew even less about the significance of their medicine bundles. As I sat across from the appointed representatives of an Alberta band, I remembered reading somewhere that eye contact was not part of Native culture.

My boss, who was unconcerned about being culturally correct, looked them right in the eye and asked them to begin. He had agreed to listen to their petition, although our department had no jurisdiction over the medicine bundles. They made their presentation and I took notes.

Susie was sitting on my shoulder, laughing at me, because I was affected by the earnestness of their request. "Don't be fooled," she said. "They're negotiating. And they know just how to make bleeding hearts like you squirm." I tried to brush her off, angry that her cynicism had rubbed off on me. We advised the delegation to approach the museum directly, knowing full well they wanted to meet with the minister and not with an ethnologist who might view them as living artefacts instead of real people with a legitimate grievance.

"Thank you for your time," they said, not meeting our eyes. I was glad that eye contact wasn't part of their culture. I couldn't have met theirs.

I have now reached observer status with my own people. When an uncle died, I went to his funeral, the first time I'd been in a Catholic church in many years. Looking at my cousins (I have twenty-four on my mother's side of the family), their spouses, and their children and stepchildren, I reflected on the real break between our generation and that of our parents. We had moved away from the parish, many of us had married (or remarried) non-French Canadians, we had had much smaller families. The homogeneity was gone, the expectations of our parents forever altered.

The funeral Mass, instead of reminding me of the rituals of my childhood, seemed remote, uninteresting. My detachment surprised me, hurt me. What about being French, being Catholic, being Canadian, all bound together? Belonging being everything?

One of my most haunting memories is of a small clapboard church on a hill in eastern Iceland and the young girl who took me there. I saw the church from my guest-house room, its steeple barely visible above the mist. After supper, I went for a walk, hoping I'd find a way up the rocky hillside to the church. I had never walked in thick mist before, and I found it so disorienting I turned back towards the guest-house.

I heard the pony long before I saw it, the sound of its hooves bouncing off the rocky hills on each side. I stopped on the road, thinking I'd ask the pony's rider for directions. The rider turned out to be a girl of about eight. I didn't have my phrase-book with me, but I tried out my *Gott kvöld* (good evening). She smiled. I pointed to the church and shrugged my shoulders, hoping she would understand I was trying to find the path up the hill. "Come," she said, dismounting and walking beside me. It was not an easy climb up the hill, the path was barely discernible, and I stumbled more than once. The girl never did, as sure-footed as her pony. When we reached the church, she tied the pony to the railing and held the door open for me.

It looked much the same as the other churches I had visited in Iceland. Extremely simple, a naive painting behind the altar. She chatted away in Icelandic, pointing out things I might have missed. She seemed unconcerned at being alone with a stranger, a stranger who could not even understand her.

I would have liked to stay longer but I was afraid her parents might be worried about her. We walked down the hill in silence, the pony following behind us. At the foot of the hill, she remounted her pony, waved at me, and disappeared into the mist.

Sometimes you are privileged to live more than one life, to cross over into another world, for a short time or forever. But most of us lead only one life, our own, and are destined to be mere observers of other lives.

Observation is not experience. So my interest in other cultures makes me an "anthropologist" by Susie's definition. My glimpses into other cultures are just that, glimpses. But they are also reminders – that there are many ways of seeing the world, that encountering another culture, no matter how briefly, can make us more human, more receptive to other visions of the world.

As Canadians, we have this strange obsession about ethnicity. Maybe because so many of us come from somewhere else. We always want to know about people's backgrounds, where they came from, or where their parents came from.

We seem fixated on cultural stereotypes. In spite of Québec's remarkable transformation (some say revolution) of its economy, we still think that French Canadians don't make good businessmen or businesswomen. We still categorize English Canadians as WASPs with only a derogatory intent.

In spite of all our talk about valuing "cultural diversity," we still associate Ukrainians with *perogies* and Easter eggs, the Chinese with egg rolls and coolie hats, the Germans with beer and *lederhosen*.

Stereotypes are a kind of shorthand, a natural by-product of our powers of observation. So we can't just wish them away. Even if we disposed of them all tomorrow, new ones would replace them over time. What is important is to go beyond the stereotype, to realize that the shorthand is not a substitute for the original text.

Knowing about a person's background can help you to understand only the person's background, not the person. We do not choose our ethnicity. We grow and develop beyond our backgrounds.

As individuals we have to overcome our unhealthy preoccupation with ethnicity, our tendency to stereotype. As Canadians we have to break free both from the myth of the two solitudes and from the confines of the cultural mosaic.

11. The Politics of Otherness

November 1976.

The house is finally quiet again. There are dirty dishes everywhere, empty champagne bottles, the remnants of a cake. Piles of cards and gifts. We have just celebrated the arrival of our adopted child.

I am reading the guest book, trying to savour the beauty of the day, to recall all the love and support we received while we waited for the child who would make us a family. I picture myself ten, twenty years from now, showing this guest book to my son, showing him the pictures of how we welcomed him into our world.

If my mother were alive to tell me of how I was welcomed into the family, the story would be very different. A baptism, followed by a family gathering. Everyone Catholic and French Canadian.

My son's welcoming "committee" was very different. As I look down the list of names, I am reminded of a comment one of my neighbours made this afternoon, after someone mentioned the recent election of the Parti Québécois.

I was hoping no one would mention the election, at least not in front of Al. He is a good neighbour and welcome in our home, even though his views of Québec are less than kind.

"Best thing that could have happened. Good riddance to Québec. Now we can finally be an English country," he managed before his wife poked him sharply in the ribs.

"Canada isn't an 'English' country, Al," I reminded him. "Just look around this room."

Of all the people we had invited, family, friends, neighbours, colleagues from work, more than half weren't born in Canada. And of those that were, many had a mixed background or were married to someone born in another country.

My own family is of course French. My husband, however, immigrated from Switzerland when he was twenty. My son's godmother has British grandparents on her mother's side and Russian Jewish grandparents on her father's. Her husband was born in England. My son's godfather is Ottawa Valley Irish; his wife was born in Hong Kong.

Alexis's honorary grandparents, a couple who are like second parents to me, are a "mixed" couple. She came to Canada from England as a war bride; his parents came to Alberta from Norway after the First World War. Their daughter, one of my best friends, is married to a Swede.

Another good friend is English Canadian, from Toronto; her husband was born in Holland. My high-school confidante, born in Alsace of a French mother and a German father, is married to an English Quebecker.

The couples we know all seem to be "mixed." Apart from my family, there were three other French-Canadian women; they have all married immigrants, a Hungarian, a Dane, and an American.

I keep thinking I'll run out of mixed couples but I don't. A New Zealander, married to an Englishman. A Swede, also married to an Englishman. An American married to a Russian. A Polish-American married to a French Canadian who was raised in English. An English Canadian married to a Jamaican. A French woman and her Indian husband, who once said to me, "When people ask me what I am – and believe me, in Canada it's a question often asked – I always say: 'Take your pick. I was born in Tanzania of Indian parents, went to school in England, met my wife in France, and now I am a landed immigrant in Canada.' "

These people aren't our friends *because of* their varied backgrounds. They are friends we have made individually or as a couple. Some are colleagues from work, others are friends from school. Some are neighbours, others we met through other friends. I never realized till today just how many of my friends come from somewhere else.

As I put the guest book and cards away, I stop to check my little son. Welcome to Canada, Alexis. Welcome to the United Nations.

* * *

CANADA IS A LAND OF OTHERNESS. WE DEFINE ourselves by what separates us. By language or ethnic origin: French, English, Ukrainian, Italian, Chinese, etc. Or by region: Maritimers, central Canadians, Prairie sons and daughters, Northerners. Some of us are even more specific: Newfoundlanders, Québécois, Albertans, British Columbians, Yukoners.

Our sense of otherness is so ingrained that we foist it on our immigrants when they try to shed their otherness to become Canadians. Perhaps because we cannot outgrow our obsession with English-French duality, we cannot let others choose to be Canadians. These "others" are either assigned their own hyphenated identity (whether they want it or not) or labelled English Canadians.

By being officially bilingual and officially multicultural, Canada has mixed the politics of language with the politics of culture, and created the politics of otherness.

Although the government accepted many of the recommendations of the Royal Commission on Bilingualism and Biculturalism regarding bilingualism, it rejected those calling for integration of ethnic groups into the French or English community. The commission's terms of reference regarding biculturalism had already mobilized ethnic groups into action, and as a result, book IV of the commission's report dealt exclusively with Canadian ethnicity (*The Cultural Contribution of the Other Ethnic Groups*).

When Prime Minister Trudeau announced the new policy of multiculturalism in 1971, he by-passed the commission's recommendations regarding ethnicity and focused on the cultural diversity expressed in book IV. This multicultural policy has now been enshrined into law: Bill C-93, "An Act for the preservation and enhancement of multiculturalism in Canada," or the Canadian Multiculturalism Act for short.

The 1971 decision to opt for multiculturalism instead of biculturalism had mixed reviews. It was hailed by some as an affirmation of the cultural mosaic, dismissed by others as political gimmickry aimed at the "ethnic vote." Some worried that linking official bilingualism and multiculturalism would ultimately defeat official bilingualism.

The politics of culture may not be as divisive as the politics of language but they hardly bring us together. Although many Canadians from ethnic groups other than French or English see the multiculturalism policy as a recognition of their vital contribution to Canadian society, the policy has had a mixed reaction among Canadians:

For Native peoples, Canada's promotion of other ethnic groups must seem ironic, given the fate of their own cultures and languages. It must be hard for them to understand the money and effort that is spent to preserve "heritage" languages that are still thriving in their countries of origin, when their own languages, native to the continent, are dying.

For many French-speaking Canadians, official multiculturalism only waters down the federal government's commitment to the preservation of their culture, a culture they feel is threatened as surely as the French language is.

Some Canadians argue that the policy encourages "ethnics" to stick together instead of adapting and becoming more like "real" Canadians.

Others associate multiculturalism with folk dancing and ethnic food rather than with the appreciation of diversity or respect for cultural identity.

Although well-intentioned, our multicultural policy seems to underestimate the upheaval inherent in the immigrant experience. In the words of Vivian Rakoff, one of Canada's most prominent psychiatrists, himself an immigrant from South Africa via England, "Every act of immigration is like suffering a brainstroke. One has to learn to walk again, to talk again, to move around the world again, and probably, most difficult of all, one has to learn to re-establish a sense of community."

Our multicultural approach assumes that immigrants will be able to re-establish that sense of community through their ethnicity rather than by assuming a Canadian identity. It is a rather *laissez-faire* approach to citizenship: letting immigrants integrate themselves as best they can, rather than helping them to integrate.

In Québec, there is more emphasis on the community than on the individual. Integration into the community is important because the community is considered important. Immigrants are expected to fit into the French-speaking majority and, if they have children, to send their children to French schools. This is partly due to the emphasis on community and partly due to the realities of Québec's very low birth rate and its impact on school enrolment, although English Canada has focused its interpretation on the latter reason.

According to the Canadian Multiculturalism Act, one of the policies of the federal government is to "promote the full and equitable participation of individuals and communities of all origins in the continuing evolution and shaping of all aspects of Canadian society and assist them in the elimination of any barrier to such participation." Immigrants to Québec might find these words hollow if they feel their equitable participation would be better achieved in English. Québec will argue that the equitable participation of the majority of Québécois is dependent on the primary use of French.

Although I'm uncomfortable with the coercion that seems to lurk under Québec's "integration" policies, I sometimes wonder whether the *laissez-faire* attitude in the rest of Canada is that useful to immigrants who, in most cases, are left to fend for themselves. If they're lucky, they may be helped by immigrant agencies or, if they're really lucky, by an established community of their own ethnic group.

The immigrant experience is part of the emotional baggage of many Canadians. The most traumatic aspect of that experience is the sense of dislocation that immigrants feel when they arrive in a new country. The intensity of that dislocation varies from one group to another, from one individual to another. An

American family that settles in Canada will obviously feel less dislocation than Vietnamese refugees who barely escaped with their lives and who can't speak English.

The feeling of dislocation is not limited to immigrants, however. Think of what happens to Inuit or Dene children who are sent south for health or education reasons, where they are totally removed from the world they have known.

Biculturals often share that sense of dislocation, even though they themselves haven't actually emigrated. (As a bicultural, however, I have not uprooted myself and travelled thousands of miles from my family and community to live among strangers. As much otherness as I have felt, there has always been a way back for me, to the other solitude. Immigrants can't always go back.)

My biculturalism is only one of many in this country. Our new immigrants are bicultural, and many second- and third-generation Canadians retain a certain biculturalism. Bilingualism does not always imply biculturalism. You can speak another language regularly without integrating into the culture that goes with it. Most immigrants, however, are forced by circumstances – going to school, earning a living – to become bicultural in varying degrees. They often live two lives simultaneously, their private life in the old culture, their public life in English or French, depending on which province they settled in.

I realize as I write this chapter how much of a misnomer the term *English Canadian* really is. My ex-husband, who emigrated from Switzerland and speaks English, French, German, and some Italian, hates to be called an anglophone, an English Canadian, or a Swiss-Canadian. He's Canadian, period. He told me that the first year we were together, the year he got his Canadian citizenship.

I also realize how many of my friends fall into the "other" category. The people who came to my son's celebratory brunch were representative of the friends I had made before and have made since.

They reject terms like *English Canadian* and *anglophone* just as I reject the labels *francophone*, *Franco-Ontarian*, and *francophone-hors-Québec*. Many of them have made comments about our fascination with backgrounds and hyphens.

A friend who has been in Canada for twenty-five years wonders why people still label him a Polish-American. "I was born in the States but I came up here to work, have a family. I'm no more Polish than you are. The only thing Polish about me is my name. It really bugs me when people tell me I should be excited with what's happening in Poland now. I'm interested in and worried about what's happening in Canada, with this French-English thing. That's what I'm worried about."

Another friend who was born in Hong Kong feels that she will always be Chinese first, Canadian second, as far as Canadians are concerned. They can't see past her Asian features. When she moved with her husband to a small town west of Ottawa, people kept asking her if her parents owned the Chinese restaurant, the only one in town.

It seems that the emphasis has always been, and continues to be, on our differences. We see ourselves as English or French and everyone else as "other." *Vive la différence*, but with a vengeance.

What worries me is that we may never transcend our differences, only perpetuate them. And as long as we thrive on our differences, there can be no Canada for all of us.

The tragedy for Canada may be that in recognizing two founding "nations" we can never be one nation. We can never be more than a collection of provinces with two official languages and many cultures. Perhaps that is all a nation can ever be; perhaps constitutions and systems of government only create an illusion of a nation that is more than the sum of its parts.

We believe ourselves to be a fair, open and welcoming society. We are – on paper at least. The Charter of Rights and Freedoms, the Canadian Human Rights Act, the Canadian Multiculturalism Act all attest to this. But if we are so fair, open and welcoming, how can we sell so many racist lapel pins, so many calendars that ridicule Sikhs – to name just two recent examples?

Respect for and appreciation of other cultures and races cannot be legislated, they must be fostered by each and every one of us, in our families, in our communities, in our municipalities. The government cannot legislate attitudes.

The politics of language and the politics of culture in this country do not seem to have fostered appreciation of diversity, respect for other cultures, or a sense of solidarity. Sometimes they've had the opposite effect. How can it be otherwise when they are the politics of otherness?

12. Living with Cultural Schizophrenia

I have this dream. That I've died and gone to heaven. I am greeted not by St. Peter but by a young man with Jean-Pierre written on a little halo on his shirt pocket.

"Welcome to Québec," he says, taking my computerized card.

"I thought this was heaven."

"It is," he says, "but heaven is divided into countries, just like on earth."

Great! Just what I wanted, to spend eternity with a *fleur-de-lis* tucked in my halo.

"There must be some kind of mistake. Because I don't come from Québec."

"You must be an FHQ, then. We look after those too."

"An FHQ?"

"A *francophone-hors-Québec*! Now if you'll just be patient, I'll run your card through the computer and check your status."

"Wait a minute! How did I get labelled an FHQ? I hate being called a *francophone-hors-Québec*. I'm a French Canadian."

"Boy, you must be older than you look. I never had anyone claiming to be a French Canadian before."

"I'm dead, remember? Dead people are supposed to be old. Now what are you going to do about my status?"

"Don't you want to be with your own people?"

"Where do Canadians go?"

"You mean English Canadians?"

Here we go again. Us and them, even in heaven.

"Yes," I say in exasperation, just to get an answer.

But Jean-Pierre isn't listening. He's staring at the screen in puzzlement.

"I'm sorry, Madame, but there's been a mistake. I'm afraid you'll have to check in at that counter over there. All biculturals go to limbo."

I walk over to the limbo counter. The person who takes my card has a strangely neutral face, not really a face at all. Sort of blurred. He (or is it a she?) doesn't have a name written on his/her shirt pocket, or a halo for that matter. I guess we don't need faces or names or any other definite sign of identity in limbo.

I should be grateful that I'm not being sent to hell, for sinning against the state, for being a *collaboratrice*.

Limbo! An ambiguous sanctuary for the culturally ambiguous, the perfect asylum for cultural schizophrenics.

* * *

I LIVE IN TWO CULTURES BY CHOICE, A CHOICE that comes back to haunt me whenever there is conflict between the two. Although I've learned to live with the everyday tension, I never seem prepared for the major confrontations. There have been three such confrontations in the last twenty years: the October Crisis, the referendum on sovereignty-association, the debate over the Meech Lake Accord.

With every crisis, the gulf widens and I find it more difficult to jump from one side to the other. I start to wonder if I made the right decision, whether it wouldn't be easier just to choose one side and be done with it. Move to Québec or British Columbia. Forget I ever knew the other side.

When the crisis passes and things return to normal, I forget my doubts and worries and enjoy my double life again. But every crisis leaves more debris for me to trip over, more choices to make than ever before.

I am lucky to be able to live my day-to-day life in French and English. Because I live in Ottawa, I have access to a wide variety of books, newspapers, radio and television programs, films, and live performances, in both languages. I can go into stores, restaurants, museums, galleries, and be served in French or English. I try not to think of what will happen to all this choice if Québec separates.

French-English decisions permeate my daily life. How bilingual to make my message on the answering machine, how many English and French Christmas cards to buy, what language software for the computer. I try to be practical, not to duplicate my life into French and English versions. But the guilt always lurks under the surface, the little voice that says: "Mais tu trahis ta langue!" (You're betraying your language.)

I think that living in two cultures would be a lot easier if I didn't carry so much emotional baggage about my first culture and language. The guilt that used to make me hide my English library books under the bed when I was twelve is still with me. Years of biculturalism have not dimmed the indoctrination I received as a child.

"Sois fière de ta langue."

"Le français, c'est l'âme de la patrie canadienne."

"Souviens-toi du règlement dix-sept. Souviens-toi toujours du règlement dix-sept."

That indoctrination included the notion, which is deep-rooted in French Canada, that language *is* culture. French-Canadian culture probably survived because differences in language and religion insulated it from the influences of the colonizing British. Even during my own childhood, being French, being Catholic, being Canadian were all bound together. Since the Catholic religion is no longer a strong factor in the preservation of French-Canadian culture, language is the only bulwark, the only safeguard. Hence the conviction that language is culture.

I don't believe that language is culture, although I realize how it might appear to be so. There are many definitions of culture, and my favourite is the one developed by Bernard Ostry (yes, a Canadian) in *The Cultural Connection*:

> Culture, however we define it, is central to everything we do and think. It is what we do and the reason why we do it, what we wish and why we imagine it, what we perceive and how we express it, how we live and in what manner we approach death. It is our environment and the patterns of our adaptation to it. It

is the world we have created and are still creating; it is the way
we see that world and the motives that urge us to change it. It
is the way we know ourselves and each other, it is our web of
personal relationships, it is the images and abstractions that
allow us to live together in communities and nations. It is the
element in which we live.

Culture, by this definition, encompasses language, religion,
adaptation to geography, history, personal relationships. If
culture encompasses so much, and I believe it does, then our
obsession with language, although understandable, is self-
defeating. If language were culture, then the British and the
Americans would have the same culture, the Spaniards and the
Argentineans, the French and the Algerians, etc.

My cultural fingerprinting is French Canadian and I can
never change it. Even if I stop speaking French tomorrow and
never speak it as long as I live, I will still be a French Canadian.
For me, it is an ethnic identification, not only a linguistic one.

Ethnicity is only one of many cultural identifications in
our lives, although it is probably the most important. I belong to
many different cultures and subcultures, as a woman, as a
mother, as a baby boomer, as a North American. And I know I
have more in common with other Canadians and my American
neighbours than I do with francophones from other continents.

La survivance has to a large extent depended on empha-
sizing and maintaining the differences between Canada's two
main cultures. In order to protect our French Catholic identity
we constantly had to highlight how different we were from
English Protestants. I was fifteen before I realized you could be
English-speaking *and* Catholic.

But indoctrination is only part of my problem. My guilt
has a second, more traumatic source. A decision I made years
ago, to write most of my fiction in English. Writing in another
language is not a decision many writers have to make.

At first, I wrote in both languages, refusing to commit

myself, avoiding a decision I knew was inevitable. I cursed my way with words, wishing I could exchange it for talent in music or art or dance. These art forms have languages that are universal, that cut across cultural and linguistic lines.

A sculptor can decide to use clay instead of stone, a musician to play another instrument, a dancer to switch from classical to jazz. But a writer who writes in another language feels that she is betraying her talent, that he is breaking some kind of secret code.

Now I write mostly in English and live with the guilt. The guilt is permanent, immutable, more reliable than any muse. For years, the characters I wrote about were strangely neutral, with names that could be French or English (Florence, Vincent, Julie) and no backgrounds. It's as if I couldn't face the choice I had made, that my characters, like me, had to be without identity.

But slowly I started to create French-Canadian characters and give them French names, old-fashioned names like Angéline and Émile, names with accents, so that the reader would always be reminded that the characters were French, although he was reading the story in English. Having done that, I was able to write about a Canadian woman with a Scottish background and call her Nellie, a Dutch immigrant and call her Margriet.

Now that I had forged a bicultural identity, my characters could have identities of their own, although not a double one like mine. I have yet to write about a French-English bicultural.

I write in English in spite of the fact that it's the language of the people who "conquered" my people.

I write in English because it best expresses what I want to say without changing who I am.

I write in English about my French past, about my double vision, about the way I see the world as a bicultural. French belongs to my monocultural childhood. It can only express what I felt then; it can't express what I feel now.

My friends who write in French cannot understand how I can write in English. They believe that English has compromised my talent, altered my subconscious, destroyed my deepest self. They have been so savage in their condemnation that we no longer discuss it.

"Traduire, c'est trahir," the saying goes. To translate is to betray. If translating is betraying, how can you write in one language about something that happened in another? How can you translate not words but memories?

I don't believe that language is my deepest self. My culture is my deepest self and its layers uniquely mine. The bottom layer is solid, the culture of my childhood, with its French, Catholic values. The other layers are my own experiences, as a woman, as a mother, as a writer, as a citizen of this country and of the world. My double vision is as valid as the single vision of my friends who write in only one language. My talent as vital as theirs.

Albert Camus once wrote that every artist has within his soul a single source of inspiration that nourishes who he is and what he says throughout his life (*L'envers et l'endroit*). My single source of inspiration is my sense of otherness, my double vision. And English is the language of that otherness, that double vision.

But for those who believe that language is culture, my writing in English is a rejection of my French culture. A culture under siege, especially one that bases itself on language, rejects the notion of biculturalism. Denies even the possibility.

"You can speak two or more languages but you can live in only one culture," I am repeatedly told. "You have to choose one or the other, you can't have both. A country can be bicultural, can have two cultures. But an individual cannot. He can have only one culture."

I think the vehemence of that position is based on the fact that my other culture is the culture of the "enemy," against which the French culture has struggled for so long. If I were claiming to be bicultural in French and Spanish, or French and Chinese, there would be surprise, even admiration, and eventual acceptance.

But biculturalism didn't just complicate my writing career. It had tremendous impact on the choices I made as a parent. Although I wanted my son raised in French, I was determined that he would not be saddled with the same emotional baggage I had about language.

When my son was a baby, my husband and I spoke to him only in French. Since we lived in an English neighbourhood and many of our friends were English-speaking, we knew he'd learn Canada's other official language soon enough.

One day, my son was showing off his favourite book to a guest in our home, pointing out the different animals and naming them in English. "Cat," he was saying, when I came to sit beside him. He immediately showed me the same page and said, "Le chat." This went on for several minutes, with him naming the animal in English first for our guest and repeating it in French for me. He had probably learned the English animal names from the baby-sitter who came two days a week. He was only two, but he had somehow distinguished the two languages (I thought all the words were just a jumble in his head) and the people he could use them with (in this case, English with the guest, French with his mother).

When it came time to choose a school, the French one nearest my home was full of English kids whose parents wanted them to be bilingual. It was a French school, not an immersion school, but because of declining enrolment it was accepting students regardless of their level of French. So I chose a school farther away that had standards of language proficiency and a strict French-only policy in the classroom (except for English class), the corridors, and the schoolyard. A policy that left me uneasy, although I understood the reasons for it.

When my son was about six, he started to speak to me more and more in English. He was doing what immigrant children were doing, speaking English at home instead of their mother tongue. Those children were going to an English school, however, and my son was not. His school was French, his little friends were French, and my brother, who lived with us at the time, spoke to him only in French. After a while and a bit of blackmail (a five-cent penalty for every English word) we were speaking French at home again.

Now that he is high school age, he speaks to his friends mostly in English and just rolls his eyes when I nag him to speak to them in French. This is a chronic problem in bilingual environments, the dominant language dominates.

Although I do nag him to speak more French, I'm grateful that he wasn't indoctrinated the way I was. That he doesn't think the French language is sacred. He has a great respect for language; he in fact learned a third language at the age of ten, to be able to communicate in German with his Swiss grandparents.

He is bewildered by but not drawn into the bitterness of the current French-English debate. Although he is really franco in his outlook, I think he sees himself as a Canadian first, *sans* hyphen. I was hoping this would be the norm for his generation and, in Ottawa at least, there are a lot of young people (some of them anglophone first) who fit that profile, who are bilingual and proud of it. In my day, the only bilingual kids were francophone first. But on the other side of the river, in Québec, it's a different story. Many of my friends' children speak no English and are proud of it. Defiant about it.

I thought my son would live in a Canada that would be strong and less divided, that his generation would not know the bitterness of mine. Although he can move effortlessly from French to English, that effortlessness may be wasted because he may come of age in a Canada without Québec.

My nine-year-old niece, who has a French father and an English mother, told me one day, while she was doing her homework: "Some people say French is better. Other people say English is better. So what am I supposed to think?"

My son will not inherit my biculturalism, he will forge one of his own. As will my nieces. As will many of their classmates. In a country where immigration is the only source of population growth, in a mobile society with few taboos to prevent inter-marriage, there will be more and more biculturalism, not less.

I hope my son's biculturalism will be a source of inspiration to him and not of conflict. That it will help him understand other people and the complex forces that have shaped them. That he will always be proud of who he is, of the languages he speaks, of the country he lives in.

Conclusion

Sometimes I close my eyes and reach deep down inside. I try to pierce the darkness, to find a sliver of light to guide me. I keep hoping I'll find my way back into my past. I can't believe it's all gone, that it doesn't exist somewhere in another dimension.

I wish I could walk back into my old house, just as it was then, and hear my mother reading from the newspaper at the kitchen table. Sneak up to my room and leaf through my books and personal scribblings. Look out the window and see my friends playing in the street.

It's hard to accept that the past exists only in your mind, like an old movie; that the reel can be lost, that the film can become brittle and turn to dust.

I want to run up to the stage and receive my little trophy with the red, white, and blue ribbon. I want to walk in the *Fête-Dieu* procession, wearing my *foulard de croisée*, and kneel in the schoolyard, convinced that my tights are personally protected by God. I want to stand proudly by the display of books I won at the *le Concours de français*.

I want to reach out and touch those parts of my life again. Because I was whole then, I "belonged."

* * *

THIS WAS NOT AN EASY BOOK TO WRITE. I CAME close to abandoning the project many times because it seemed too personal, too revealing. Why expose my innermost conflicts, my humble opinions and biases? Why run the risk of being branded an *assimilée* for expressing a bicultural point of view?

It's one thing to discuss my feelings with family and friends, quite another to address the world out there, a world once again hostile (some would say always) to Québec and to French Canada.

Every chapter challenged my ambivalence, every incident

stirred my guilt. I would go from feeling confident that biculturalism was an honourable choice, an achievement of some kind, to feeling that I was betraying every French Canadian who ever struggled to survive. Often within the time it took to write one paragraph.

I realize now that I have to learn to let go of my ambivalence and guilt, that I have to accept who I am instead of looking back at who I used to be.

When I reread all the incidents I have assembled for this book, I am struck by my passivity, by my cowardice. Did I really sit there in silence while those idiots made comments about frogs near the water cooler? Why didn't I report the guy who rifled through my purse and called me a frog fucker? Why did I watch quietly as the police searched Paulette's apartment only to lie about it afterwards?

Why did I let Yvon upset me with his comments about my French on that bluff in Iceland? Why have I listened in silence when my people have called me an *assimilée* or a *vendue*?

I am not a passive person. I am very articulate and vocal about my views. So who is this timid person I have been describing, this wimp who couldn't or wouldn't face her accusers?

I don't know. Some of those incidents happened twenty years ago. Maybe I was too caught up in the guilt, in the balancing act of living between cultures. Maybe I couldn't risk rocking the proverbial boat. I no longer have that problem.

In always trying to understand two cultures, I have run the risk of not understanding myself. By living in two cultures, I have learned not to belong in spite of the fact that I come from a culture where belonging is everything.

I remember a discussion I had once with some artists in Halifax. They were discussing art and life, and how artists have to separate themselves from the community in order to create their art. I told them how impossible that was for me, that in my culture, belonging was everything.

"Your writing should be everything. If you need to belong, then you have no business being an artist."

"But I come from a culture where belonging is everything," I repeated lamely, ashamed to hear a hint of a whine in my voice. They looked at each other, shrugged collectively, and started to talk about the high cost of studio space. I concluded that they just didn't understand, that they came from a culture that didn't place much (or enough) emphasis on belonging.

Now I realize that belonging is not a state of grace that can be granted or taken away. That the kind of cultural security I am looking for is internal, not external. That no one has rejected me or taken away my right to belong. That my sense of not belonging has been rooted in my own ambivalence, my own rejection of who I am.

Because I grew up in a society under siege, a society that sought refuge in its history and institutions in order to survive, I felt I had no right to belong once I set foot outside its walls.

By hanging on to my ambivalence, to my guilt, to my sense of not belonging, I have avoided the reality of what I have done, which is to step into another cultural mould, one of my own making. I need to acknowledge and take responsibility for what I have become, which is a bilingual, bicultural Canadian.

Cultural boundaries are never easy to cross, but to travel back and forth is probably more difficult than crossing once and never looking back. The friends of my childhood have crossed those boundaries in a number of different directions. Some have turned their backs on French culture to raise their children in English; others have moved to Québec to raise their children in a French-only environment. Many have stayed in Ontario to raise their children in French, like their parents and grandparents before them.

I choose to live and raise my child in both cultures. This is considered one step away from assimilation and is strongly discouraged. I think of it as becoming Canadian, and I am grateful for the incredible richness it has brought to my life. A richness I want to share with my son.

My bilingualism allows me to witness every major Canadian event, in person or through the media, and understand every word that is said, every nuance, without interpreters. To travel across Canada and appreciate the history, traditions, and diversity of this vast country. To travel the rest of the world, knowing that my fellow Canadians have come from every corner of the globe.

To read the best Canadian literature, whether it was written in French or English or in another language that has been translated. To have access to the literature of two great civilizations, the French and the British and their many colonies-turned-nations as well as English and French translations of the literature of other countries.

To explore other languages, each of which brings me new insights, new ideas, new ways of looking at the world.

To gain insight into other cultures and how they shape people and their responses to the past and present.

So if I had a choice, I wouldn't change it.

When I was very young, I fancied myself to be an internationalist. I joined a United Nations Club, read books and pamphlets on world government, tried to study Esperanto. As an adult, my focus narrowed. I became a Canadian nationalist, particularly in terms of our economy and our cultural autonomy. But I now find my focus widening again, my interest in internationalism rekindled.

With environmental, humanitarian, and economic concerns drawing nations closer together, I want Canada to face the twenty-first century, not only intact but ready to confront the globalization that is taking place.

We as Canadians depend on one another. Just when the world is consolidating into larger entities we could be breaking up an entity that is too small in the first place. Canada may be vast, may rank as the second-largest country in the world, but our population is only slightly bigger than that of the State of California.

Canadians have been crossing cultural boundaries for generations and will continue to do so in the future. The ethnic and racial mix of our population is changing. Instead of facing that reality, we fuss over our fragile identity and cling to our cultural clichés. When our immigrants try to become Canadians, to be part of our present and future, we ignore them, to stare into our two distinct versions of the past.

It's not first- or second-generation Canadians who are tearing this country apart, but Canadians whose roots go much deeper. We are fighting over the past instead of fighting for the future.

We all have to let go of our guilt and ambivalence, our sense of not belonging. We have to let go of the past. We have to step into another national mould, one of our own making. We have to acknowledge and take responsibility for what we have become, for being Canadians.

Printed in Canada